Records of Emigrants from England and Scotland to North Carolina 1774-1775

EDITED BY A. R. NEWSOME

Reprinted from the *North Carolina Historical Review 11*
(January and April 1934)

Printed by Edwards Brothers Inc.

INTRODUCTION

Pursuant to a letter from John Robinson, secretary of the Treasury, December 8, 1773, customs officials in England and Scotland supplied lists of persons who took passage on ships leaving Great Britain during the years 1773-1776, giving names, ages, quality, occupation, employment, former residence, reasons for emigrating, and the name of the vessel and master. These records, somewhat incomplete as now preserved in the Public Record Office of Great Britain under the classification Treasury Class 47, Bundles 9-12, contain many thousands of names and important information on a remarkable population movement which was of great significance to America and of arresting attention to the landed and manufacturing interests and the government of Great Britain.[1] They have been printed in part in *The New England Historical and Genealogical Register* (1908-1911).

The largest group consisted of indented servants bound for New York, Pennsylvania, Maryland, and Virginia; and the next largest, of emigrants sailing from ports in northern England to Nova Scotia, Virginia, and New York. The emigration practically ceased after September, 1775. The movement from Scotland was due chiefly to the oppressive rent policy of the Highland proprietors and middlemen of the region extending from Ayr County to the Shetland Islands. A traveler on an emigrant ship in 1774 wrote: "It is needless to make any comment on the conduct of our Highland and Island proprietors. It is self-evident what consequences must be produced in time from such numbers of subjects being driven from the country. Should levies be again necessary, the recruiting drum may long be at a loss to procure such soldiers as are now aboard this vessel."[2]

---

[1] *Acts of the Privy Council of England, Colonial Series*, V, 340.
[2] Charles M. Andrews, *Guide to the Materials for American History, to 1783, in the Public Record Office of Great Britain*, II, 224-5.

However, in the war which began a year later between England and the American colonies, many of the Highlanders were loyal to England and from them was recruited the Royal Highland Regiment. Economic conditions were of paramount importance in driving the emigrants from England and Scotland and in luring them to the New World.

With less attractive economic conditions, North Carolina did not receive so large a share of the new settlers, particularly those from England, as did Virginia, Maryland, Pennsylvania, or New York. The mass movement to North Carolina was more pronounced among the Scotch Highlanders, due partly to the fact that since about 1739 many of their kinsmen had already settled on the Cape Fear in the counties of Cumberland, Bladen, and Anson. In 1770 the General Assembly, in behalf of about sixteen hundred Highlanders who had landed in the province during the past three years, passed an act exempting settlers who came direct from Europe from the payment of all taxes for a term of four years.[3] At the outbreak of the Revolution, the estimated number of Scotch Highlanders in North Carolina was 15,000.[4]

The compilation here printed is from transcripts in the North Carolina Historical Commission of the selected records of those emigrants whose destination was North Carolina.

The list of emigrants from England to North Carolina contains about one hundred names. There are nearly three times as many males as females, and the average recorded age of the entire group is twenty-five years. Twenty-three are listed as indented servants, of whom three are women, nine are indented for four years, and two for two years. The chief group consists of artisans from the cities of England. Several pleasure-seekers and six family groups are noted.

Nearly five hundred names are in the lists from Scotland. There are nearly one hundred family groups. The males exceed the females in the ratio of about three to two, and there are seventy children without sex designation. The average recorded age is twenty-five years. The majority consists of farmers and laborers from the Highland counties of Argyle, Sutherland, and

[3] Acts of the Privy Council of England, Colonial Series, V. 340.
[4] R. D. W. Connor, Race Elements in the White Population of North Carolina, 57.

Caithness. Low wages, high rents, low prices of cattle, high prices of bread due to distilling, the conversion of farm lands into sheep pastures, and the exactions of landlords at home, added to the reputation of Carolina for high wages, cheap land, and plentiful provisions, account largely for the emigration.

RECORDS OF EMIGRANTS FROM ENGLAND[5]

An Account of all Persons who have taken their passage on Board any Ship or Vessel, to go out of this Kingdom from any Port in England, with a description of their Age, Quality, Occupation or Employment, former residence, to what Port, or place they propose to go, & on what Account, & for what purposes they leave the Country[6]

FROM JANUARY 15 TO JANUARY 23, 1774

Embarked from the Port of London

William Wilson, 38, Planter, London, Carolina, Carolina, Jnº. Besnard, as a planter.

Benjamin Blackburn, 28, Clergyman, London, Carolina, Carolina, Jnº. Besnard, to settle there.

Robert Rose, 20, Planter, London, Carolina, Carolina, Jnº. Besnard, as a planter.

George Ogier, 15, Planter, London, Carolina, Carolina, Jnº. Besnard, as a planter.

Robt. Knight, 26, Planter, London, Carolina, Carolina, Jnº. Besnard, as a planter.

Henry Chapman, 30, Jeweller, London, Carolina, Carolina, Jnº. Besnard, to work at his Business.

Henry Maskal, 19, Clerk, London, Carolina, Carolina, Jnº. Besnard, as a Clerk.

John Williams, 30, Cabinet Maker, London, Carolina, Carolina, Jnº. Besnard, for Employment.

Thomas Vernan, 22, Silk Throwster, London, Carolina, Carolina, Jnº. Besnard, for Employment.

Embarked from the Port of Falmouth[7]

Colin Campbell, ..., ..., Carolina, Le De Spencer (Packet Boat), Capt. Pond, no further Account.

Custom House London, 15th February 1774. Exd. Jnº. Tomkyns.[8]

---

[5] These records are compiled from transcripts in the North Carolina Historical Commission of selections from emigration lists in Treasury Class 47, Bundle 9, in the Public Record Office of Great Britain.

[6] The information concerning each emigrant, in the order given, is classified in the original reports under the following headings: names; age; quality, occupation or employment; former residence; to what port or place bound; by what ship or vessel; master's name; for what purposes they leave the country.

[7] A port in Cornwall in southwest England.

[8] Endorsed: "Sixth Week Account of the Emigration."

3

Embarked from the Port of London

William Scott, 21, Malster, Scotland, North Carolina, Margaret & Mary, Saml. Tzatt, for Employment.

Margaret Scott, 16, Spinster, Scotland, North Carolina, Margaret & Mary, Saml. Tzatt, for Employment.

William Sim, 24, Husbandman, Scotland, North Carolina, Margaret & Mary, Saml. Tzatt, for Employment.

Jane Sim, 24, Wife to William Sim, Scotland, North Carolina, Margaret & Mary, Saml. Tzatt, for Employment.

David Marshal, 24, Clerk, Scotland, North Carolina, Margaret & Mary, Saml. Tzatt, as a Clerk.

James Blakswik, 21, Clerk, Scotland, North Carolina, Margaret & Mary, Saml. Tzatt, as a Clerk.

David Wilson, 38, Merchant, London, Carolina, Union, W^m. Combs, on Business.

John Macklin, 24, Gentleman, Oxford, Carolina, Union, W^m. Combs, to Settle.

Mary Macklin, 23, Wife to John Macklin, Oxford, Carolina, Union, W^m. Combs, to Settle.

Lewis Ogier, 47, Weaver, London, Carolina, Union, W^m. Combs, to Settle.

Catherine Ogier, 40, Wife to the above, London, Carolina, Union, W^m. Combs, to Settle.

Thomas Ogier, 20, Silk Throwster, London, Carolina, Union, W^m. Combs, to Settle.

Lewis Ogier, 19, Silk Throwster, London, Carolina, Union, W^m. Combs, to Settle.

Catherine Ogier, 16, Spinster, London, Carolina, Union, W^m. Combs, to Settle.

Lucy Ogier, 13, Spinster, London, Carolina, Union, W^m. Combs, to Settle.

Charlotte Ogier, 9, Spinster, London, Carolina, Union, W^m. Combs, to Settle.

John Ogier, 8, School Boy, London, Carolina, Union, W^m. Combs, to Settle.

Mary Ogier, 6, Spinster, London, Carolina, Union, W^m. Combs, to Settle.

Peter Ogier, 5, School Boy, London, Carolina, Union, W^m. Combs, to Settle.

Custom House London, 22^d April 1774. Ex^d. Jno. Tomkyns.[9]

---

[9] Endorsed: "The Eleventh Week's Emigration Account."

FROM MARCH 21 TO MARCH 28, 1774

Embarked from the Port of Liverpool

John Edward, 26, Farmer, Cheshire, South Carolina, Polly, ..., To Farm.

Jane Edward, 27, his Wife, Cheshire, South Carolina, Polly, ..., going with her Husband.

William Simpson, 43, Cooper, B Lincolnshire, South Carolina, Polly, ..., To Trade.

James Wilson, 18, Sadler, Bedfordshire, South Carolina, Polly, ..., To Trade.

James Clark, 42, Butcher, Middlesex, South Carolina, Polly, ..., To Trade.

William Walker, 37, Merchant, Yorkshire, South Carolina, Polly, ..., To Trade.

Custom Ho: London, 28th May 1774. Exd. Jno. Tomkyns.[10]

FROM APRIL 19 TO APRIL 26, 1774

Embarked from the Port of London

Janet Belton, 20, Spinster, London, Carolina, Magna Charta, Rd. Maitland, going to her Friends.

Tobiah Blackett, 25, Spinster, London, Carolina, Magna Charta, Rd. Maitland, going to her Friends.

Custom H. London, 22d. June 1774. Exd. Jno. Tomkyns.[11]

FROM MAY 10 TO MAY 17, 1774

Embarked from the Port of London

John Grafton, 25, Drawing Master, London, Carolina, Briton, Alexr. Urquhart, on Business.

Nathaniel Worker, 25, Gentleman, London, Carolina, Briton, Alexr. Urquhart, on Pleasure.

Custom Ho. London, 5th July 1774. Exd. Jno. Tomkyns.[12]

FROM MAY 17 TO MAY 24, 1774

Embarked from the Port of London

Mary Bands, 35, Widow, Herts, North Carolina, Friendship, John Smith, Indented Servant for Four Years.

Mary Kenneday, 21, Spinster, Scotland, North Carolina, Friendship, John Smith, Indented Servant for Four Years.

John Brown, 21, Book keeper, Birmingham, North Carolina, Friendship, John Smith, Indented Servant for Four Years.

George Taverner, 21, Groom, Southwark, North Carolina, Friendship, John Smith, Indented Servant for Four Years.

[10] Endorsed: "The Fifteenth Week of the Emigration Account."
[11] Endorsed: "The Nineteenth Week of the Emigration Account."
[12] Endorsed: "The Twenty-Second Week of the Emigration Account."

Embarked from the Port of London

Edward Gilks, 22, Leather dresser, Coventry, North Carolina, Friendship, John Smith, Indented Servant for Four Years.

John Forster, 24, Printer, London, North Carolina, Friendship, John Smith, Indented Servant for Four Years.

Thomas Winship, 26, Clockmaker, Reading, North Carolina, Friendship, John Smith, Indented Servant for Four Years.

John Darby, 40, Baker, London, North Carolina, Friendship, John Smith, Indented Servant for Four Years.

William Andrews, 31, Carpenter, Surry, North Carolina, Friendship, John Smith, Indented Servant for Four Years.

Custom H°. London, 13 July 1774. Ex^d. Jn°. Tomkyns.[13]

FROM MAY 24 TO MAY 31, 1774

Embarked from the Port of London

Miss Tong, 16, Spinster, London, Carolina, Pallas, J. Turner, going on Pleasure.

M^r. Ginnings, 25, Clerk, London, Carolina, Pallas, J. Turner, as Clerk to a Merchant.

M^rs. Molley, 30, ..., London, Carolina, Pallas, J. Turner, going to her Husband.

Custom H°. London, 13th. July 1774. Ex^d. Jn°. Tomkyns.[14]

FROM JULY 10 TO JULY 17, 1774

Embarked from the Port of London

Sarah White, 56, Merchant, London, Carolina, Carolina, Jn°. Besnard, going on Business.

John Detlaf, 30, Taylor, London, Carolina, Carolina, Jn°. Besnard, going to Settle.

Sarah Detlaf, 25, Wife of John Detlaf, London, Carolina, Carolina, Jn°. Besnard, going to Settle.

Custom H°. London, 15 August 1774. Ex^d. Jn°. Tomkyns Assist: Insp^r. Genl.[15]

FROM JULY 31 TO AUGUST 7, 1774

Embarked from the Port of London

John Butler, 25, Gentleman, London, Carolina, Carolina Packet, John White, going to Settle.

Ann Butler, 25, Wife of John Butler, London, Carolina, Carolina Packet, John White, going to Settle.

[13] Endorsed: "The Twenty-Third Week of the Emigration Account."
[14] Endorsed: "The Twenty-Fourth Week of the Emigration Account."
[15] Endorsed: "The Thirty-First Week of the Emigration Account."

FROM JULY 31 TO AUGUST 7, 1774—*continued*

Embarked from the Port of London

Thomas Andrews, 35, Potter, London, Carolina, Carolina Packet, John White, going to Settle.

William Templeman, 28, Jeweller, London, Carolina, Carolina Packet, John White, going to Settle.

John Smith, 22, Cabinet Maker, London, Carolina, Carolina Packet, John White, going to Settle.

Custom H°. London, 31ˢᵗ. August 1774. Exᵈ. Jn°. Tomkyns, Assist: Inspʳ. Genˡ.[16]

FROM AUGUST 14 TO AUGUST 21, 1774

Embarked from the Port of London

David Adkins, 22, Cooper, Lincoln, Carolina, William, Philip Wescott, Indented Servant.

James Nichols, 24, Silver Caster, London, Carolina, William, Philip Wescott, Indented Servant.

Thomas Winter, 21, Husbandman, Leicester, Carolina, William, Philip Wescott, Indented Servant.

John Rixon, 22, Brazier & Copper Smith, Birmingham, Carolina, William, Philip Wescott, Indented Servant.

Benjamin Evans, 22, Sail Cloth Weaver, Cornwall, Carolina, William, Philip Wescott, Indented Servant.

John Anthony, 21, Baker, Middlesex, Carolina, William, Philip Wescott, Indented Servant.

James Smith, 21, Painter & Glazier, Nottingham, Carolina, William, Philip Wescott, Indented Servant.

Michael Delancy, 21, Husbandman, Ireland, Carolina, William, Philip Wescott, Indented Servant.

Custom House London, 24ᵗʰ Octob- 1774. Exᵈ. Jn°. Tomkyns Assist: Inspʳ. Genˡ.[17]

FROM OCTOBER 3 TO OCTOBER 10, 1774

Embarked from the Port of London

Rachael L'Fabuere, 40, Lady, London, ... Curling, going for Pleasure.

Jane Bignell, 47, Servant of Rachael L'Fabuere, London, Carolina, London, ... Curling, going with Mʳˢ L'Fabeure.

Ann Bowie, 36, Servant of Rachael L'Fabeure, London, Carolina, London, ... Curling, going with Mʳˢ L'Fabeure.

Elizᵃ. Batty, 16, a native of Carolina, London, Carolina, London, ... Curling, going home.

Ann Weston, 30, Lady, London, Carolina, London, ... Curling, going for pleasure.

16 Endorsed: "The Thirty-Fourth Week of the Emigration Account."
17 Endorsed: "Emigration Account. No. 36."

Embarked from the Port of London

John West, 28, Gentleman, London, Carolina, London, ... Curling, going for pleasure.

John Auldjo, 15, Gentleman, London, Carolina, London, ... Curling, going for pleasure.

Alex^r. Auldjo, 16, Gentleman, London, Carolina, London, ... Curling, going for pleasure.

Robert Dee, 33, Gentleman, London, Carolina, London, ... Curling, going for pleasure.

Henry Houseman, 35, Gentleman, London, Carolina, London, ... Curling, going for pleasure.

Embarked from the Port of Newcastle

Thomas Stead, 17, Butcher, Hull, Cape Fear, Rockingham, Richard Hopper, going to his Father, who lives there.

Custom H°. London, 10th Novemb. 1774. Ex^d. Jn°. Tomkyns Assist: Insp^r. Genl.[18]

FROM OCTOBER 17 TO OCTOBER 24, 1774

Embarked from the Port of London

Stephen Eglin, 25, Draper, London, Carolina, Newmarket, Gilbert Wilson, going to settle.

Jasper Scouler, 30, Carpenter, London, Carolina, Newmarket, Gilbert Wilson, going to settle.

Robt. Maxwell, 18, Clerk, Scotland, Carolina, James, Isaac Thompson, going to settle.

Willson Dabzall, 25, Jeweller, Scotland, Carolina, James, Isaac Thompson, going to settle.

Bezabeer Forsyth, 22, Gentleman, Scotland, Carolina, James, Isaac Thompson, going to settle.

Sarah Eastwood, 16, Spinster, London, South Carolina, Lowther, Thos. Cowman, Indented Servant.

Joseph Dyer, 21, Waiter, London, South Carolina, Lowther, Thos. Cowman, Indented Servant.

William Kenneday, 25, Peruke Maker, London, South Carolina, Lowther, Thos. Cowman, Indented Servant.

Ralph Richardson, 35, Gardener, Surry, South Carolina, Lowther, Thos. Cowman, Indented Servant.

Custom H°. London, 5th Decemb. 1774. Ex^d. Jn°. Tomkyns. Assist: Insp^r. Genl.[19]

---

[18] Endorsed: "Emigration Account. No. 43."
[19] Endorsed: "Emigration Account. No. 45."

Embarked from the Port of London

William Ripley, 22, Farmer, York, Carolina, Mary & Hannah, Henry Dixon, going to Settle.

John Sanderson, 45, Farmer, York, Carolina, Mary & Hannah, Henry Dixon, going to Settle.

John Blythe, 32, Gentleman, London, Carolina, Mary & Hannah, Henry Dixon, on Pleasure.

James Flatt, 25, Taylor, London, Carolina, Mary & Hannah, Henry Dixon, Indented Servant for two years.

James Trenham, 22, Butcher, York, Carolina, Mary & Hannah, Henry Dixon, Indented Servant for two years.

Custom H°. London, 5th December 1774. Exd. Jn°. Tomkyns Assist: Inspr. Genl.[20]

From November 28 to December 6, 1774

Embarked from the Port of London

John Mackenzie, 16, Clerk & Bookkeeper, Scotland, Carolina, Briton, Alexr. Urquhart, going to settle.

Alexander Douglas, 22, Husbandman, Scotland, Carolina, Briton, Alexr. Urquhart, going to settle.

Christopher Smith, 49, Husbandman, Switzerland, Carolina, Briton, Alexr. Urquhart, going to settle.

Esther Smith, 35, Wife to the above, Switzerland, Carolina, Briton, Alexr. Urquhart, going to settle.

Andrew Milborn, 7, Child, Switzerland, Carolina, Briton, Alexr. Urquhart, going to settle.

Christopher Milborn, 2, Child, Switzerland, Carolina, Briton, Alexr. Urquhart, going to settle.

Custom H°. London, 13th Janry 1775. Exd. Jn°. Tomkyns Assist: Inspr. Genl.[21]

---

[20] Endorsed: "Emigration Account. No. 48."
[21] Endorsed: "Emigration Account. No. 51."

RECORDS OF EMIGRANTS FROM SCOTLAND[22]

R. E. Philips to John Robinson

Sir

In obedience to your Letter of the 8th. of December 1773, I am directed to enclose to You, Lists of Persons, who have taken their Passage from the Ports of Port Glasgow[23] and Kirkaldy,[24] for North America on board the Ships Commerce and Jamaica Packet, for the Information of the Right Honorable the Lords Commissioners of His Majesty's Treasury.

Customhouse Edinburgh   R. E. Philips
        20th. June 1775

Port Kirkaldy An Account of Emigration from this Port and precinct to America or other Foreign Ports from the 5th. of June 1775, to the 11th. do. both inclusive.

Emigrants on board the Jamaica Packet of Burntisland[25] Thomas Smith master for Brunswick North Carolina.

> Miss Elizabeth Mills & her servant going to reside in So. Carolina from Dundee.[26]

> John Durmmond & John Marshall Coopers from Leith,[27] goes out because they get Wages than in their own Country.

> John Douglas Labourer from Dundee, goes out for the above Occasion John Mills and Thomas Hill Joiners from Do. go to settle in So. Carolina.

> Andrew Williamson, James Jamaison & William Mitchell Farmers & Fishermen from Schetland[28] with their Wives & seven Children.

Farmers and Fishermen go abroad because the Landholders in Schetland have raised their rents so high that they could not live without sinking the little matter they had left.   Total 20 Passengers.

N.B. no other Emigration from this Port or precinct in the Course of this week.

Signed { Robert Whyt Collr:
        { Philip Paton Compr:

---

[22] These records are compiled from transcripts in the North Carolina Historical Commission of selections from emigration lists in Treasury Class 47, Bundle 12, in the Public Record Office of Great Britain, under the title, "Lists of Emigrants from Scotland to America with letters from Comers. of Customs in Scotland touching the sailing of the Emigrant Ships, 1774-5."
[23] In Renfrew County on the River Clyde.
[24] In Fife County across the Firth of Forth from Edinburgh.
[25] Near Kirkcaldy.
[26] In Forfar County on the eastern coast.
[27] Near Edinburgh.
[28] The Shetland Islands off the northern coast of Scotland.

Port Stranraer,[29] An Account of Emigrants shipped at Stranraer the 31st May 1775 on board the Jackie of Glasgow James Morris Master for New York in North America, with a Description of their Age, Quality, Occupation, Employment, Former Residence, On what Account and for what purposes they leave the Country.[30]

25, Jaˢ. Matheson, 38, Labourer, New Luce,[31] North Carolina, In hopes of good Employment.

26, Jean McQuiston, 27, ..., New Luce, North Carolina, ...

27, Margᵗ. Matheson, 4, ..., New Luce, North Carolina, ...

28, Jnº. McQuiston, 46, Labourer, Inch,[31] North Carolina, In hopes of better Employmᵗ.

29, Cathr: Walker, 46, ..., New Luce, North Carolina, For a better way of doing.

36, Jaˢ. McBride, 38, Farmer, New Luce, North Carolina, The High rent of Land.

37, Janet McMiken, 39, ..., New Luce, North Carolina, ...

38, Archᵈ. McBride, 7, ..., New Luce, North Carolina, ...

39, Eliz: McBride, 5, ..., New Luce, North Carolina, ...

40, Jenny McBride, 4, ..., New Luce, North Carolina, ...

61, Jaˢ. Steven, 27, Farmer, Inch, Nº. Carolina, In hopes of better Bread.

62, Chrⁿ. Steven, 23, ..., Inch, Nº. Carolina, with her Brother.

63, Sarah Steven, 16, ..., Inch, Nº. Carolina, with her Brother.

64, Thoˢ. Steven, 11, ..., Inch, Nº. Carolina, with his Brother.

65, Jnº. Dalrymple, 40, Farmer, New Luce, Nº. Carolina, The High Rent of Land.

66, Marg. Gordon, 39, ..., New Luce, Nº. Carolina, ...

67, Mary Dalrymple, 19, ..., New Luce, Nº. Carolina, ...

68, Jn. Dalrymple, 17, ..., New Luce, Nº. Carolina, ...

69, Archᵈ. Dalrymple, 15, ..., New Luce, Nº. Carolina, ...

70, Jaˢ. Dalrymple, 11, ..., New Luce, Nº. Carolina, ...

71, Ann Dalrymple, 9, ..., New Luce, Nº. Carolina, ...

72, Janet Dalrymple, 7, ..., New Luce, Nº. Carolina, ...

73, Jean Dalrymple, 5, ..., New Luce, Nº. Carolina, ...

74, Wᵐ. Dalrymple, 2, ..., New Luce, Nº. Carolina, ...

29 On Loch Ryan in Wigtown County in southwestern Scotland.
30 In the order here given, the information is classified in the original report under the following headings: number, emigrants' names, ages years, occupation or employment, former residence, to what port or place bound, on what account and for what purposes they leave the country.
31 Near Stranraer.

Port Stranraer—*continued*

75, Alex^r. McBride, 22, Labourer, New Luce, N°. Carolina, In hopes of better Employment.

78, John Duff, 20, A Herdsman, New Luce, N°. Carolina, In hopes of good Employ^t.

79, Wm Eckles, 40, Shoemaker, Inch, N°. Carolina, In hopes of good Business.

80, Martha McKenzie, 45, ..., Inch, N°. Carolina, ...

81, John Eckles, 12, ..., Inch, N°. Carolina, ...

Customh°. Stranraer 5 June 1775.

N.B. As all the Married Women follow their Husbands and the Children their parents, We have inserted no Reason, for their leaving the Country, after their Names.

John Clugston Collr.
Polk McIntire
Comp.

R. E. Philips to John Robinson

Sir,

In obedience to your Letter of the 8th. of December 1773, I am directed to inclose to you, a List of Persons who have taken their Passage from the Port of Greenock,[32] for North America, on board the Ship Christy Hugh Rellie Master bound to New York, and Georgia, and the Ship Ulysses James Wilson Master bound for North Carolina, for the Information of the Right Honorable the Lords Commissioners of His Majestys Treasury.

Customhouse Edinburgh, 8th May 1775.   R. E. Philips

Port Greenock List of Passengers from the 28th April 1775, Inc^l. to the 5 May 1775 Exclusive, [by the Ulysses James Wilson Master for North Carolina].[33]

Math. Lyon, 49, Weaver, Glasgow,[34] Want of Employ.

Mary Lyon, his spouse, 50, ..., Glasgow, ...

James Lyon, 21, Weaver, Glasgow, Want of employ.

John Kennburgh, 24, Labourer, Glasgow, Want of employ.

James Kennburgh, 27, Labourer, Glasgow, Want of employ.

John McNabb, 24, Labourer, Argyleshire,[35] Want of employ.

Jean Campbell his Spouse, 19, ..., Argyleshire, ...

Tebby McNabb, 20, to get a husband, Argyleshire, ...

Doug. McVey, 30, Labourer, Argyleshire, Want of employ.

James Buges, 27, Merchant, Edinb., to follow his business.

Marg. Hog his spouse, 25, to comfort her husband, Edinb., ...

Ed. Penman D Coll^r
John McVicar D Comp

---

[32] In Renfrew County near Port Glasgow.
[33] The information in the order given here is classified in the original report under the headings: names, age, occupation, former place of residence, reasons for emigration.
[34] In Lanark County on the River Clyde.
[35] On the western coast of Scotland.

R. E. Philips to John Robinson

Sir

In obedience to your Letter of the 8th of December 1773, I am directed to inclose to you, a List of Persons who have taken their Passage from the Port of Greenock, for North America, on board the Ship Monimia Edward Morrison Master, bound for New York, and the Ajax Robert Cunningham Master for North Carolina, for the Information of the Right Honorable the Lords Commissioners of His Majestys Treasury.

Custom house Edinburgh   R. E. Philips
8th June 1775

List of Passengers from the 26th of May 1775 Inclusive to the 2[d] June 1775 Exclusive.[36]

Walter Mcfarlane, 20, Gentleman, To be a Merchant, North Carolina, In the Ajax Robert Cunningham Master.

Mary Menzies, 25, Lady, Going to her Husband, ..., In the Ajax Robert Cunningham Master.

Signed { Edward Penman D. Collector
John McVicar D. Comp[r]
John Dunlop Tide Surveyor

Commissioners of the Customs in Scotland to John Robinson

Sir,

The inclosed Paper is a List of Persons lately sailed as Emigrants, to Wilmington in North Carolina, from the Port of Greenock, which We transmit to you Sir, for the Information of the Right Honorable the Lords Commissioners of the Treasury.

Charterhouse Edinburgh, 22 August 1774. { Arch[d] Menzies
George Clerk Maxwell
Basil Cochrane

List of Passengers on board the Ship Ulysses James Chalmers Mas[r] for Wilmington in North Carolina.[37]

Robe[t] McNicol, 30, Glenurcha,[38] Gent[n], High Rents and oppression.

Jean Campbell, 24, Glenurcha, his wife, ...

Annapel McNicol their Daug., 8, Glenurcha, ...

Abram Hunter, 28, Greenock, Shipmas., To Build.

Thomas Young, 21, Glasgow, Surgeon, To follow his Trade.

John McNicol, 24, Glenurcha, Workman, High rents & oppression.

---

[36] The information in the order given is classified in the original report under the headings: names, age, occupation, on what account and for what purpose they go, to what place bound, in what ship they take their passage.

[37] The information in the order given is classified in the original report under the headings: passengers' names, age, former place of residence, business, reasons for emigrating.

[38] In Argyle County on the western coast of Scotland.

Angus Galbreath, 30, Glenurcha, Workman, Poverty Occasioned by want of work.

Katrine Brown his wife, 26, ..., ..., Poverty Occasioned by want of work.

Angus Fletcher, 40, Glenurcha, Farmer, High rents & Oppression.

Katrine McIntyre his wife, 40, Glenurcha, ..., High rents & Oppression.

Euphame Fletcher, 10, Glenurcha, their child, High rents & Oppression.

Mary Fletcher, 6, Glenurcha, their child, High rents & Oppression.

Nancy Fletcher, 3, their child, High rents & Oppression.

John McIntyre, 45, Glenurcha, Farmer, High rents & Oppression.

Mary Downie, 35, Glenurcha, his wife, High rents & Oppression.

Nancy McIntyre, 11, Glenurcha, their child, High rents & Oppression.

Don^d McIntyre, 8, Glenurcha, their child, High rents & Oppression.

Christy McIntyre, 5, Glenurcha, their child, High rents & Oppression.

John McIntyre, 4, Glenurcha, their child, High rents & Oppression.

Duncan McIntyre, 40, Glenurcha, Farmer, High rents & Oppression.

Katrine McIntyre, 28, Glenurcha, his wife, High rents & Oppression.

John Sinclair, 32, Glenurcha, Farmer, High rents & Oppression.

Mary Sinclair, 32, Glenurcha, his wife, High rents & Oppression.

Donald McIntyre, 28, Glenurcha, Farmer, High rents & Oppression.

Mary McIntyre, 25, Glenurcha, his wife, High rents & Oppression.

Don^d McFarlane, 26, Glenurcha, Farmer, High rents & Oppression.

Don^d McFarlane, 6, Glenurcha, his son, High rents & Oppression.

Duncan Sinclair, 24, Glenurcha, Farmer, High rents & Oppression.

Isobel McIntyre, 24, Glenurcha, his wife, High rents & Oppression.

John McIntyre, 35, Glenurcha, Farmer, High rents & Oppression.

Marg^t. McIntyre, 30, Glenurcha, his wife, High rents & Oppression.

Malcolm McPherson, 40, Glenurcha, Farmer, High rents & Oppression.

Christ^n Downie, 30, Glenurcha, his wife, High rents & Oppression.

Janet McPherson, 10, Glenurcha, their child, High rents & Oppression.

Willm. McPherson, 9, Glenurcha, their child, High rents & Oppression.

Willm. Picken, 32, Glenurcha, Farmer, High rents & Oppression.

Martha Huie, 26, Glenurcha, his wife, High rents & Oppression.

Robt Howie, 18, Glenurcha, Workman, Poverty Occasion'd by want of work.

Arc^d McMillan, 58, Glenurcha, Farmer, High rents & Oppression.

Mary Taylor, 40, Glenurcha, his wife, High rents & Oppression.

Barbra McMillan, 20, Glenurcha, their Daug^r, High rents & Oppression.

John Greenlees, 25, Kintyre,[39] Farmer, High rents & Oppression.
Mary Howie, 25, Kintyre, his wife, High rents & Oppression.
Peter McArthur, 58, Kintyre, Farmer, High rents & Oppression.
Chirs^t Bride, 52, Kintyre, his wife, High rents & Oppression.
John McArthur, 16, Kintyre, their child, ...
Ann McArthur, 38, Kintyre, their child, ...
Jean McArthur, 20, Kintyre, their child, ...
John McArthur, 28, Kintyre, their child, ...
Danl Calewell, 18, Kintyre, Shoemaker, Poverty Occasion'd by want of work.
Robt Mitchell, 26, Kintyre, Taylor, Poverty Ocasion'd by want of work.
Ann Campbell, 19, Kintyre, his wife, Poverty Ocasion'd by want of work.
Alex^r Allan, 22, Kintyre, Workman, Poverty Ocasion'd by want of work.
Iver McMillan, 26, Kintyre, Farmer, High rents & Opression.
Jean Huie, 23, Kintyre, his wife, High rents & Opression.
John Ferguson, 19, Kintyre, Workman, Poverty Occasiond by want of work.
Rob McKichan, 32, Kintyre, Farmer, High rents & Opression.
Janet McKendrick, 24, Kintyre, his wife, High rents & Opression.
Neil McKichan, 5, Kintyre, their son, High rents & Opression.
Mal^m McMullan, 58, Kintyre, Farmer, High rents & Opression.
Cath^n McArthur, 58, ..., his wife, ...
Daniel McMillan, 24, ..., Farmer their child, High rents & Opression.
Arch^d McMillan, 16, ..., their child, High rents & Opression.
Gelb^t McMillan, 8, ..., their child, ...
Don^d McKay, 20, ..., Taylor, High rents & Opression.
Danl Campbell, 25, ..., Farmer, High rents & Opression.
And^w Hyndman, 46, ..., Farmer, High rents & Opression.
Cath^n Campbell, 46, ..., his wife, High rents & Opression.
Mary Hindman, 18, ..., their child, High rents & Opression.
Marg^t Hyndman, 14, ..., their child, High rents & Opression.
Angus Gilchrist, 25, ..., their child, High rents & Opression.
Mal^m Smith, 64, ..., Farmer, High rents & Opression.
Mary McAlester, 64, ..., his wife, High rents & Opression.
Peter Smith, 23, ..., their child, High rents & Opression.
Mary Smith, 19, ..., their child, High rents & Opression.
Duncan McAllum, 22, ..., Shoemaker, High rents & Opression.
Cath^n McAlester, 30, ..., his wife, High rents & Opression.
Neil Thomson, 23, ..., Farmer, High rents & Opression.
David Beaton, 28, ..., Farmer, High rents & Opression.
Flora Bride, 29, ..., his Wife, High rents & Opression.
John Gilchrist, 25, ..., Cooper, High rents & Opression.

---

[39] In Argyle County on the western coast.

Marion Taylor, 21, ..., his wife, High rents & Opression.
Neil McNeil, 64, ..., Farmer, High rents & Opression.
Isobel Simpson, 64, ..., his wife, High rents & Opression.
Danl McNeil, 28, ..., their child, High rents & Opression.
Hector McNeil, 24, ..., their child, High rents & Opression.
Peter McNeil, 22, ..., their child, High rents & Opression.
Neil McNeil, 18, ..., their child, High rents & Opression.
Willm McNeil, 15, ..., their child, ...
Mary McNeil, 9, ..., their child, ...
Allan Cameron, 28, ..., Farmer, High rents & Opression.
Angus Cameron, 18, ..., Farmer, High rents & Opression.
Katrine Cameron, 21, ..., his wife, High rents & Opression.

Alex Campbell D Com^r   Jo Clerk D. Coll^r
P^t Greenock   John Dunlop T S

The above List of Passengers is from the 12th August 1774 Inc^l. to the 18th Augt 1774 Inc^l.

Commissioners of the Customs in Scotland to John Robinson
Sir

We have herewith transmitted a Copy of a Letter from the principal Officers of the Customs at Campbelton,[40] giving an Account of a Ship touching there, from Greenock, with Emigrants taken on board in the Island of Isla,[41] which, if judged requisite, you will be pleased to lay before the Lords Commissioners of His Majestys Treasury.

M Cardonnel
George Clerk Maxwell
Basil Cochrane

Customh°. Edinb^g
3^d. Jany 1775

Ronald Campbell and Archibald Buchanan to Commissioners of Customs in Scotland

Customhouse Campbelton
12th December 1774

Honourable Sirs,

In obedience to your Letter of the 15th of December 1773, We beg leave to acquaint your Honours that the Brigantine Carolina Packet Malcolm McNeil Master, with Goods from Greenock for Cape Fair in North Carolina, was put into this Harbour by a contrary wind on the 2^d. and sailed on the 7th. instant, having on board sixty two Passengers, of whom thirty were men, fifteen Women, and seventeen Children; This Ship after sailing from Greenock, called at Lochindale in Isla, where the Passengers were taken on board, part of whom belonged to the Island of Isla, and part to the Island of Mull[42] who had come to Isla, to take their Passage.

---

[40] In Argyle County, near Kintyre.
[41] Islay Island in Argyle County.
[42] In Argyle County, north of Islay Island.

By the best accounts we could get, only five of these Passengers were People of any consequence the rest were of a lower class, Servants of these Gentlemen, or Labourers who could pay for their Passage. We are &c^a.

Signed { Ronald Campbell
Arch^d Buchanan

Commissioners of the Customs in Scotland to John Robinson

Sir

The Officers of the Customs in the Islands of Schetland in consequence of the Instructions received from hence, having particularly examined sundry Emigrants for America, put into Schetland by Distress of Weather; We have inclosed the said Examinations, (Copies of them) as containing apparently the genuine Causes of many Persons leaving the Country, and going to America, desiring you will lay the same before the Lords Commissioners of the Treasury for their Information.

Customh^o. Edin^g., 30th May 1774.

Arch^d Menzies
George Clerk Maxwell
Basil Cochrane

Port Lerwick[43]

Report of the Examination of the Emigrants from the Counties of Caithness and Sutherland[44] on board the Ship Bachelor of Leith bound to Wilmington in North Carolina.

William Gordon saith that he is aged sixty and upwards, by Trade a Farmer, married, hath six children, who Emigrate with him, with the Wives and Children of his two sons John & Alexander Gordon. Resided last at Wymore in the Parish of Clyne in the County of Sutherland, upon Lands belonging to William Baillie of Rosehall. That having two sons already settled in Carolina, who wrote him encouraging him to come there, and finding the Rents of Lands raised in so much that a Possession for which his Grandfather paid only Eight Merks Scots he himself at last paid Sixty, he was induced to emigrate for the greater benefit of his children being himself an Old Man and lame so that it was indifferent to him in what Country he died. That his Circumstances were greatly reduced not only by the rise of Rents but by the loss of Cattle, particularly in the severe Winter 1771. That the lands on which he lived have often changed Masters, and that the Rents have been raised on every Change; and when Mr Baillie bought them they were farmed with the rest of his purchase to one Tacksman[45] at a very high Rent, who must also have his profits out of them. All these things concurring induced him to leave his own country in hopes that his Children would earn their Bread more comfortably elsewhere. That one of his sons is a Weaver and another a Shoe Maker, and he hopes they may get bread for themselves and be a help to support him.

---

[43] In the Shetland Islands.
[44] Caithness and Sutherland counties constitute the northern end of Scotland.
[45] A middleman who leased a large piece of land from the owner and sublet it in small farms.

William McKay, aged Thirty, by Trade a Farmer, married, hath three children from Eight to two years Old, besides one dead since he left his own country, resided last at —————— in the Parish of Farr in the County of Strathnaver upon the Estate of the Countess of Sutherland. Intends to go to Wilmington in North Carolina, because his stock being small, Crops failing, and bread excessively dear, and the price of Cattle low, he found he could not have bread for his Family at home, and was encouraged to emigrate by the Accounts received from his Countrymen who had gone to America before him, assuring him that he might procure a Comfortable Subsistence in that country. That the land he possessed was a Wadset of the Family of Sutherland to Mr Charles Gordon of Skelpick, lying in the height of the country of Strathnaver, the Rents were not raised.

W^m. Sutherland, aged Forty, a Farmer, married, hath five children from 19 to 9 years old, lived last at Strathalidale in the Parish of Rea, in the County of Caithness, upon the Estate of the late Colonel McKay of Bighouse; Intends to go to North Carolina; left his own country because the Rents were raised, as Soldiers returning upon the peace with a little money had offered higher Rents; and longer Fines or Grassums,[46] besides the Services were oppressive in the highest degree. That from his Farm which paid 60 Merks Scots, he was obliged to find two Horses and two Servants from the middle of July to the end of Harvest solely at his own Expence, besides plowing, Cutting Turf, making middings,[47] mixing Dung and leading it out in Seed time, and besides cutting, winning, leading and stacking 10 Fathoms of Peats yearly, all done without so much as a bit of bread or a drink to his Servants.

John Catanoch, aged Fifty Years, by Trade a Farmer, married, hath 4 Children from 19 to 7 years old; resided last at Chabster in the Parish of Rae, in the County of Caithness, upon the Estate of M^r. Alex^r. Nicolson, Minister at Thurso, Intends to go to Wilmington North Carolina; left his own Country because crops failed, Bread became dear, the Rents of his Possession were raised from Two to Five Pounds Sterling, besides his Pasture or Common Grounds were taken up by placing new Tennants thereon, especially the grounds adjacent to his Farm, which were the only grounds on which his Cattle pastured. That this method of parking and placing Tenants on the pasture Grounds rendered his Farm useless, his Cattle died for want of Grass, and his Corn Farm was unfit to support his Family, after paying the Extravagant Tack duty. That beside the rise of Rents and Scarcity of bread, the Landlord exacted arbitrary and oppressive Services, such as obliging the Declarant to labour up his ground, cart, win, lead and stack his Peats, Mow, win and lead his Hay, and cut his Corn and lead it in the yard which took up about 30 or 40 days of his servants and Horses each year, without the least Acknowledgement for it, and without Victuals, save the men that mowed the Hay who got their Dinner only. That he was induced to Emigrate by Advices received from his Friends in

46 A premium paid to a feudal superior on entering upon the holding.
47 Manure heaps.

18

America, that Provisions are extremely plenty & cheap, and the price of labour very high, so that People who are temperate and laborious have every Chance of bettering their circumstances- Adds that the price of Bread in the Country he hath left is greatly Enhanced by distilling, that being for so long a time so scarce and dear, and the price of Cattle at the same time reduced full one half while the Rents of lands have been raised nearly in the same proportion, all the smaller Farms must inevitably be ruined.

Eliz: McDonald, Aged 29, unmarried, servant to James Duncan in Mointle in the Parish of Farr in the County of Sutherland, Intends to go to Wilmington in North Carolina; left her own country because several of her Friends having gone to Carolina before her, had assured her that she would get much better service and greater Encouragement in Carolina than in her own Country.

Donald McDonald, Aged 29 years, by Trade a Farmer and Taylor, married, hath One Child six years Old. Resided last at Chapter in the Parish of Rae in the County of Caithness upon the Estate of Mr Alex^r Nicolson Minister at Thurso, intends to go to Carolina; left his own Country for the reasons assigned by John Catanoch, as he resided in the same Town and was subjected to the same Hardships with the other. Complains as he doth of the advanced price of Corn, owing in a great measure to the consumption of it in Distilling.

John McBeath Aged 37, by Trade a Farmer and Shoe maker, Married, hath 5 children from 13 years to 9 months old. Resided last in Mault in the Parish of Kildonnan in the County of Sutherland, upon the Estate of Sutherland. Intends to go to Wilmington in North Carolina; left his own country because Crops failed, he lost his Cattle, the Rent of his Possession was raised, and bread had been long dear; he could get no Employment at home, whereby he could support himself and Family, being unable to buy Bread at the prices the Factors on the Estate of Sutherland & neighboring Estates exacted from him. That he was Encouraged to emigrate by the Accounts received from his own and his Wife's Friends already in America, assuring him that he would procure comfortable subsistence in that country for his Wife and Children, and that the price of labour was very high. He also assigns for the Cause of Bread being dear in his Country that it is owing to the great quantities of Corn consumed in brewing Risquebah.

James Duncan, Aged twenty seven years, by Trade a Farmer, married, hath two Children, one five years the other 9 Months old. Resided last at Mondle in the Parish of Farr in the Shire of Sutherland, upon the Estate of Sutherland, Intends to go to Wilmington in North Carolina; left his own Country because Crops failed him for several years, and among the last years of his labouring he scarce reaped any Crop; Bread became dear and the price of Cattle so much reduced that One Cows price could only buy a Boll[48] of Meal. That the People on the Estate of Sutherland were often supplied with meal from

---

[48] A measure of 6 bushels generally in Scotland.

Caithness, but the Farmers there had of late stopt the sale of their Meal, because it rendered them a much greater Profit by Distilling. That he could find no Employment at home whereby he could support his Family. That he has very promising Prospects by the Advices from his Friends in Carolina, as they have bettered their circumstances greatly since they went there by their labours. Lands being cheap and good Provisions plenty, and the price of Labour very encouraging.

Hector Mcdonald, Aged 75, Married, a Farmer, hath three sons who emigrate with him, John Alexander & George from 27 to 22 years old, also two Grand Children Hector Campbell aged 16, and Alex^r Campbell aged 12, who go to their Mother already in Carolina. Resided last at Langwall in the Parish of Rogart in the County of Sutherland, upon the Estate of Sutherland. Intends to go to North Carolina, Left his own Country because the Rents of his possession had been raised from One pound seven shillings to Four pounds, while the price of the Cattle raised upon it fell more than One half, and not being in a Corn Country the price of Bread was so far advanced, that a Cow formerly worth from 50sh. to £ 3 - could only purchase a Boll of Meal. He suffered much by the death of Cattle, and still more by oppressive Services exacted by the factor, being obliged to work with his People & Cattle for 40 days and more Each year, without a bit of Bread. That falling into reduced Circumstances he was assured by some of his children already in America that his Family might subsist more comfortably there, and in all events they can scarce be worse. Ascribes the excessive price of corn to the consumption of it in distilling.

William McDonald, Aged 71, by Trade a Farmer married hath 3 children from 7 to 5 years Old, who emigrate with him. Resided last at little Savall in the Parish of Lairg in the county of Sutherland, upon the Estate of Hugh Monro of Achanny. Intends to go to Wilmington in North Carolina; left his own Country because Crops failed, Bread became dear, the Rents of his possession were raised, but not so high as the Lands belonging to the neighboring Heritors, by which and the excessive price of Meal, the lowness of the price of Cattle, and still further by a Cautionary[49] by which he lost 30 £ Sterling, his Circumstances were much straightened, so that he could no longer support his Family at Home, tho' M^r. Monro used him with great humanity. That his Friends already in Carolina, have given him assurance of bettering his condition, as the price of labour is high and Provisions very cheap. Ascribes the high price of Corn to the Consumption of it in Distilling.

Hugh Matheson, Aged 32, married, hath 3 children from 8 to 2 years Old, also a Sister Kathrine Matheson aged 16, who emigrate with him, was a Farmer last at Rimsdale in the Parish of Kildonan in the County of Sutherland, Leaves his Country and goes to Carolina, be-

---

49 Personal security.

cause upon the rise of the price of Cattle some years ago the Rent of his Possession was raised from £ 2.16.0 to £ 5.10.0. But the price of Cattle has been of late so low, and that of Bread so high, that the Factor who was also a Drover would give no more than a Boll of Meal for a Cow, which was formerly worth from 50 sh to 3 £ and obliged the Tenants to give him their Cattle at his own price. That in these grassing Counties little Corn can be raised, and for some years past the little they had was in a great measure blighted and rendered useless by the frost which is common in the beginning of Autumn in the Inland parts of the Country. That in such Circumstances it seems impossible for Farmers to avoid Ruin, and their distresses heighten'd by the consumption of corn in distilling in a Grassing Country where little can be raised. That encouraged by his Friends already in America, he hath good hopes of bettering his Condition in that Country.

Willm. McKay, Aged 26, Married, a Farmer last at Craigie in the Parish of Rae and County of Caithness, upon the Estate of George McRay Island handy;[50] Goes to Carolina because the Rent of his Possession was raised to double at the same time that the price of Cattle was reduced one half, and even lower as he was obliged to sell them to the Factor at what price he pleased; at the same time his Crope was destroyed by bad Harvests, and Bread became excessive dear, owing in a great measure to the Consumption by distilling. That the Services were oppressive, being unlimited and arbitrary, at the pleasure of the Factor, and when by reason of sickness the Declarant could not perform them he was charged at the rate of one shilling p day. He had Assurances from his Friends in America that the high price of labour and cheapness of Provisions would enable him to support himself in that Country.

Alex. Sinclair, Aged 36, Married, hath 3 children from 18 to 2 years Old, a Farmer last at Dollochcagy in the Parish of Rae and County of Caithness, upon the Estate of Sir John Sinclair of Murkle. Left his own Country and goes to Carolina, because the Tacksman of Sr John Sinclair's Estate, demanded an advanced Rent and Arbitrary Services, which in the present Distresses of the Country could not be complied with without ruin. That he is encouraged by his Friends in America to hope to better his Circumstances there.

George Grant, Aged twenty, Married, a Farmer last at Aschog in the Parish of Kildonan in the County of Sutherland on the Estate of ————— Intends to go to North Carolina, because Crops failed so that he was obliged to buy four months Provisions in a year, and at the same time the price of Cattle was reduced more than One half. That his Brothers in Law, already in America have assured him that from the Cheapness of Provisions, and the high price of labour, he may better his Circumstances in that Country.

---

50 Handa Island off the western coast of Sutherland County.

William Bain, Aged 37, a Widower, by Trade a Shopkeeper, resided last in Wick in the County of Caithness. Intends to go to Carolina. Left his own Country because he could not get bread in his Employment, the Poverty of the Common People with whom he dealt disabling them to pay their debts. Hopes to better his Condition in America, but in what business he cannot determine till he comes there.

George Morgan, Aged 37, Married, hath two children. One 7 the other One year Old, a Farmer last at Chabster in the Parish of Rae, and County of Caithness, upon lands belonging to M^r. Alex^r. Nicolson Minister at Thurso. Goes to Carolina leaving his country for the same reasons and upon the same Motives assigned by John Catanoch, who was his Neighbour. See Pages 3^d & 4th of this Report.

Willm Monro, Aged thirty four, Married, Emigrates with his Wife, a servant maid, and a servant Boy, by Trade a Shoemaker, resided last at Borgymore in the Parish of Tongue, and County of Sutherland. Left his own Country as his Employment was little and he had no hopes of bettering his Circumstances in it, which he expects to do in America.

Patrick Ross, Aged thirty five Unmarried, lately Schoolmaster in the Parish of Farr, in the County of Sutherland. Goes to America on the Assurance of some of his Friends already in that Country of procuring a more profitable School for him.

Alex^r. Morison, Aged Sixty, Married, hath One Son and a Servant Maid, who emigrate with him; resided last at Kinside in the Parish of Tongue and County of Sutherland, on the Estate of Sutherland, by Occupation a Farmer. Left his Country as the Rents of his Possession were near doubled, the price of Cattle low, and little being raised in that Country, what they bought was excessive dear, beside the Tenans were in various ways opprest by Lord Raes Factors; and by the Reports from America he is in hopes of bettering his Circumstances in that Country.

George McKay, Aged 40, Married, hath one Child, a year old, by Trade a Taylor and Farmer, last at Strathoolie in the Parish of Kildonan and County of Sutherland, upon that part of the Estate of Sutherland set in Tack to George Gordon by whom his rent was augmented, and great Services demanded, vizt 12 days work yearly over and above what he paid to the Family of Sutherland. That the price of Cattle on which he chiefly depended was greatly reduced, and the little Corn raised in the Country almost totally blighted by Frost for two years past, by which the Farmers in general were brought into great distress. In these Circumstances he had no resource but to follow his Countrymen to America as the condition can scarce be worse.

Donald Gun, Aged thirty three, married, hath three Children from 8 years to 5 weeks old, by Trade a Taylor, resided last at Achinnaris in the Parish of Halerick in the County of Caithness. Finding he cannot make bread in his own Country, intends to go to America in hopes of doing it better there.

John Ross, Aged 47, a Widower hath six Children, from 20 to 5 years Old, who emigrate with him, by Trade a Farmer, last at Kabel in the Parish of Farr and County of Sutherland, upon the Estate of Sutherland. Goes to Carolina, because the rent of his Possession was greatly Advanced the price of Cattle which must pay that Rent reduced more than one half, and bread which they must always buy excessively dear. The evil is the greater that the Estate being parcelled out to different Factors and Tacksmen, these must oppress the subtenants, in order to raise a profit to themselves, particularly on the Article of Cattle, which they never fail to take at their own prices, lately at 20/ or 20 Merks, and seldom or never higher than 30/ tho' the same Cattle have been sold in the Country from 50 to 55 sh. By these means reduced in his circumstances, And encouraged by his Friends already in America, he hopes to live more comfortably in that Country.

James Sinclair, Aged twenty one years, a Farmer, married, hath no Children, resided last at Forsenain in the Parish of Rea, and County of Caithness, upon the Estate of Bighouse now possest by George McRay of Islandhanda, upon a Farm, paying 8 £ Sterling Rent, that he left his own Country because Crops of Corn had, and Bread was very dear; he had lost great part of his Cattle two years ago, the rearing Cattle being his principal business, the prices of Cattle were reduced one half while the Rents were nevertheless kept up and in many places advanced. In such Circumstances it was not possible for people of small stock to evite ruin. His Father, Mother and Sisters and some other Friends go along with him to Carolina, where he is informed land and Provisions are cheap, labour dear, and Crops seldom fail. What employment he shall follow there he hath not yet determined, but thinks it will be Husbandry.

Aeneas McLeod, Aged sixty, a Farmer, married, hath one Daughter 15 years Old. Resided last in the Parish of Tongue in the County of Sutherland upon the Estate of Lord Rae. Goes to Wilmington in North Carolina, where he proposes to live by day labour, being informed that one days Wages will support him a week. Left his own Country because upon the rise of the price of Cattle some years ago, the Rent of his Possession was raised from 28/ to 38/ a year, but thereafter when the price of Cattle was reduced one half the Rent was nevertheless still kept up. Moreover being near the house of Tongue, He was harrassed and oppressed with arbitrary Services daily called for without Wages or Maintenance.

Aeneas Mackay, Aged twenty, single, resided last with his Father in the Parish of Tongue and county of Sutherland; hath been taught to read, write and cypher, and goes to Carolina in hopes of being employed either as a Teacher or as a Clerk; He has several Relations and Acquaintances there already, who inform him he may get from 60 to 70 £ a year in this way, which is much better than he had any reason to expect at home.

Donald Campbell, Aged 50, a Farmer, married, has one Son 12 years Old, resided last in the Parish of Adrahoolish, in the County of Sutherland on the Estate of Rea. Intends to go to Carolina because the small Farm he possest could not keep a Plough, and he could not raise so much Corn by delving as maintain his Family and pay his Rent, which was advanced from 21/ to 30/. Has hopes of meeting an Uncle in America who will be able to put him in a way of gaining his Bread.

W^m McRay, Aged 37, a Farmer, married, has four Children from 8 years to 18 Months old; and one man Servant, who emigrate with him; resided last at Shathaledale in the Parish of Rea, and County of Caithness upon the Estate of George McRay of Bighouse. Left his Country because the Rent of his Possession was raised from 30 to 80 £ Scots, while at the same time the price of Cattle upon which his subsistence and the payment of his Rent chiefly depended had fallen in the last Seven years at least one half. In the year 1772 he lost of the little Crop his Farm produced and in Cattle to the value of 40 £ Sterling – under these loses and discouragements, he had assurances from a Brother and Sister already in Carolina, that a sober industrious man could not fail of living comfortably, Lands could be rented cheap, and Grounds not cleared purchased for 6 d. an Acre, that the soil was fertile, and if a man could bring a small Sum of Money with him he might make rich very fast. He proposes to follow Agriculture but has not yet determined, whether he will purchase or rent a Possession.

Willm McLeod, Aged twenty six, a Farmer, married, has one Son two years old; resided last in the Parish of Adrachoolish, in the County of Sutherland, upon the Estate of Bighouse; intends to go to Wilmington in North Carolina, where he has a Brother settled who wrote him to come out assuring him that he would find a better Farm for him than he possest at home (the rent of which was considerably raised upon him) for One fourth of the Money, and that he will live more comfortably in every respect.

Hugh Monro, Aged twenty-six, a Shoemaker, married, hath no children. Resided last in the Parish of Tongue and County of Sutherland. Goes to Carolina upon assurance that Tradesmen of all kinds will find large Encouragement.

Willm. Sutherland Aged twenty four, married, left an only Child at home. Resided last in the Parish of Latheron and County of Caithness, upon the Estate of John Sutherland of Forse. Goes to Carolina because he lost his Cattle in 1772, and for a farm of 40/ Rent, was obliged to perform with his Family and his Horses so many and so arbitrary services to his Landlord at all times of the year, but especially in Seed time & Harvest, that he could not in two years he possest it, raise as much Corn as serve his Family for six months That his little Stock daily decreasing, he was encouraged to go to Carolina, by the Assurances of the fertility of the land, which yields three Crops a year, by which means Provisions are extremely cheap, Wheat being sold at 3 shill^s. a Boll, Potatoes at 1 Sh so that one Mans labour will maintain a Family of Twenty Persons. He has no Money, therefore proposes to employ himself as a Day labourer, his Wife can spin & Sew, and he has heard of many going out in the same way who are now substantial Farmers. At any rate he comforts himself in the hopes that he cannot be worse than he has been at home.

James McKay, Aged 60, a shoemaker, married, has one child, Resided last on Lord Raes Estate in Strathnaver. Left his own country, being exceeding poor, and assured by his Friends who contributed among them the money required to pay for his Passage, that he would find better employment in Carolina.

This and the 20 preceding Pages contain the Examination of the Emigrants on board the Ship Batchelor of Leith, Alex^r Ramage Master, taken by the officers at the Port of Lerwick.

15th April 1774.

———————

A List of Passengers or Emigrants on Board the Ship Jupiter of Larne Samuel Brown Master for Wilmington in North Carolina, their Names, Ages, Occupations or Employments and former Residence.[51]

1, John Stewart, 48, Clothier, Glenurchy.
2, Elizabeth, 46, his wife, Glenurchy.
3, John Stewart, 15, their son, Glenurchy.
4, Margaret, 13, their Daughter, Glenurchy.
5, Janet, 12, their Daughter, Glenurchy.
6, Patrick Stewart, 6, their son, Glenurchy.
7, Elizabeth, 3, their Daughter, Glenurchy.
8, Donald MacIntire, 54, Labourer, Glenurchy.
9, Katherine, 41, His Wife, Glenurchy.
10, Mary, 12, their Daughter, Glenurchy.
11, Margaret, 9, their Daughter, Glenurchy.
12, John McIntire, 6, their son, Glenurchy.
13, Duncan McIntire, 5, their son, Glenurchy.
14, William Campbell, 28, Labourer, Glenurchy.
15, Katherine, 32, His Wife, Glenurchy.
16, Robert Campbell, 2, His Son, Glenurchy.
17, Duncan Campbell, ————, His Son an Infant, Glenurchy.
18, Donald Mac Nichol, 40, Labourer, Glenurchy.

---

[51] The information in the order given is classified in the original report under the headings: number, names, ages, occupation or employment, former residence.

19, Katherine, 33, His Wife, Glenurchy.

20, John McNicol, 6, their son, Glenurchy.

21, Nicol McNicol, 4, their son, Glenurchy.

22, Archibald McNicol, 2, their son, Glenurchy.

23, Mary, ————, their daughter an Infant, Glenurchy.

24, John McIntire, 35, Labourer, Glenurchy.

25, Ann, 32, His Wife, Glenurchy.

26, Margaret, 6, their Daughter, Glenurchy.

27, Archibald McIntire, 4, their Son, Glenurchy.

28, John McIntire, ————, their Son an Infant, Glenurchy.

29, Archibald Stewart, 30, Shoemaker, Glenurchy.

30, Ann Sinclair, 65, Spinster, Glenurchy.

31, Margarit her Daugh^r., 25, Spinster, Glenurchy.

32, Ann McIntire, 60, Spinster, Glenurchy.

33, Christian Downy, 25, Spinster, Glenurchy.

34, Katherine McVane, 30, Spinster, Glennurchy.

35, Mary Downie, 4, her daughter, Glennurchy.

36, Joseph Downie an Infant, ————, her son, Glennurchy..

37, Dugal McCole, 38, Labourer, Glennurchy.

38, Ann, 38, his Wife, Glennurchy.

39, Marget, 10, their Daughter, Glennurchy.

40, Mary, 8, their Daughter, Glennurchy.

41, Sarah, 2, their Daughter, Glennurchy.

42, An Infant, ————, ————, Glennurchy.

43, Angus McNicol, 30, Labourer, Glennurchy.

44, Ann, 20, His Wife, Glennurchy.

45, Dougald Stewart, 40, Labourer, Glenurchy.

46, His Wife, 40, Labourer, Glenurchy.

47, John Stewart, 16, their son, Glenurchy.

48, James Stewart, 10, their son, Glenurchy.

49, Thomas Stewart, 6, their son, Glenurchy.

50, Alexander Stewart, 4, their son, Glenurchy.

51, Allan Stewart, 44, Late Lieut^t. in Frasers Regiment, Apine.[52]

52, Donald Carmichail, 22, His servant, Apine.

53, Lilly Stewart, 7, his natural Daugh^r., Apine.

54, Alexander Stewart, 35, Gentleman Farmer, Apine.

55, Charles Stewart, 15, His Son, Apine.

56, John McCole, 49, Labourer, Apine.

57, Mildred McCole, 40, His Wife, Apine.

58, John McCole, 16, their son, Apine.

59, Samuel McCole, 15, their son, Apine.

60, Donald McCole, 12, their son, Apine.

61, Dougald McCole, 8, their son, Apine.

62, Alexander McCole, 4, their son, Apine.

---

[52] In Argyle County.

63, Katherine, 2, their Daughter, Apine.
64, Evan Carmichael, 40, Labourer, Apine.
65, Margaret, 38, His Wife, Apine.
66, Archibald Carmichael, 14, their Son, Apine.
67, Allan Carmichael, 12, their Son, Apine.
68, Katherine, 3, their Daughter, Apine.
69, Duncan McCole, 35, Farmer, Apine.
70, Christian, 35, His Wife, Apine.
71, Dugald McCole, 20, Their son, Apine.
72, Christian, 2, their Daughter, Apine.
73, Katherine, 3, their Daughter, Apine.
74, Malcolm McInish, 40, Labourer, Apine.
75, Jannet, 36, His Wife, Apine.
76, John McInish, 20, Their son, Apine.
77, Ann, 15, Their Daughter, Apine.
78, Catherine, 11, Their Daughter, Apine.
79, Donald McInish, 8, their Son, Apine.
80, Archibald McInish, 4, their Son, Apine.
81, Kenneth Stewart, 40, late Ship Master, Apine.
82, Isobel, 30, His Wife, Apine.
83, Alexander Stewart, 14, their Son, Apine.
84, John Stewart, 5, their Son, Apine.
85, Banco Stewart, 3, their Son, Apine.
86, Christian, 3, their Daughter, Apine.
87, William an Infant, ————, their son, Apine.
88, Mary Black, 16, their Servant, Apine.
89, Christian Carmichael, 14, their Servant, Apine.
90, John Black, 14, their Servant, Apine.
91, Dugald Carmichael, 55, Farmer, Apine.
92, Mary, 55, His Wife, Apine.
93, Archibald Colquhoun, 22, her Son, Apine.
94, Ann Colquhoun, 20, her Daughter, Apine.
95, Donald McCole, 34, Labourer, Apine.
96, Katherine, 40, his Wife, Apine.
97, Evan McCole, 6, their son, Apine.
98, John McIntire, 32, Taylor, Alpine.
99, Katherine, 30, his Wife, Alpine.
100, Donald McIntire, 3, their son, Alpine.
101, John McIntire, 1, their son, Alpine.
102, Gilbert McIntire, 34, Taylor, Alpine.
103, Ann, 36, his Wife, Alpine.
104, Charles McIntire, 11, their Son, Alpine.
105, Margaret, 9, their Daughter, Alpine.
106, Evan McIntyre, 5, their Son, Alpine.
107, Malcolm McIntire, 1, their Son, Alpine.
108, Duncan McCole, 45, Farmer, Alpine.

109, Christian, 40, His Wife, Alpine.

110, Duncan McCole, 21, His son, Alpine.

111, Mary, 18, their Daughter, Alpine.

112, Sarah, 15, their Daughter, Alpine.

113, Christian, 10, their Daughter, Alpine.

114, Mildred, 6, their Daughter, Alpine.

115, Ann, 3, their Daughter, Alpine.

116, Donald Black, 45, Labourer, Lismore.[53]

117, Jannet, 34, His Wife, Lismore.

118, Christian, 8, his Daughter, Lismore.

119, Ann, 4, his Daughter, Lismore.

120, Ewen, 4, their Son, Lismore.

121, Duncan, 1¾, their Son, Lismore.

122, Archibald Carmichael, 26, Labourer, Lismore.

123, Mary, 26, His Wife, Lismore.

124, Catherine, 7, their Daughter, Lismore.

125, Lachlan McLaren, 25, Labourer, Apine.

126, Lawrine McLarine, 20, Joiner, Apine.

127, Donald McLaren, 12, Labourer, Apine.

128, Duncan McLaren, 30, Labourer, Apine.

129, David McCole, 30, Labourer, Apine.

130, Duncan McIntire, 55, Labourer, Apine.

131, Katherine, 55, His Wife, Apine.

132, May, 24, Their Daughter, Apine.

133, Katherine, 17, Their Daughter, Apine.

134, Elizabeth, 14, Their Daughter, Apine.

135, Miss Christy McDonald, 25, Symstress, Apine.

136, Duncan McCallum, 30, Labourer, Apine.

Reasons assigned by the Persons named on this and y[e] three preceeding Pages of this List for their Emigrating follows Viz[t]. The Farmers and Labourers who are taking their Passage in this Ship Unanimously declare that they never would have thought of leaving their native Country, could they have Supplied their Families in it. But such of them as were Farmers were obliged to quit their Lands either on account of the advanced Rent or to make room for Sheepherds. Those in particular from Apine say that out of one hundred Mark Land that formerly was occupied by Tennants who made their Rents by rearing Cattle and raising Grain, Thirty three Mark Land of it is now turned into Sheep Walks and they seem to think in a few years more, Two thirds of that Country, at least will be in the same State so of course the greatest part of the Inhabitants will be obliged to leave it. The Labourers Declare they could not Support their families on the Wages they earned and that it is not from any other motive but the dread of want that they quit a Country which above all others they would wish

[53] In Argyle County.

to live in. Captain Allan Stewart formerly a Lieutenant in Frasers Regiment goes with an Intention of settling in the Lands granted him by the Government at the End of last War. But should the Troubles continue in America he is Determined to make the Best of his way to Boston and Offer his Services to General Gage.

The Tradesmen have a prospect of getting better Wages but their principal reason seems to be that their relations are going and rather than part with them they chuse to go along.

Signed { Duncan Campbell Collector
         { Neil Campbell Comptroller

September 4th. 1775.

Port Greenock List of Passengers from this Port from the 8th September 1774 inclusive, to the 15th September 1774 exclusive, [in the Diana, Dugald Ruthven for North Carolina].[54]

William McDonald, Kintyre, Farmer, 40, Wilmington North Carolina, For High Rents & better Encouragement.

Isobel Wright, Kintyre, ————, 36, Wilmington North Carolina, For High Rents & better Encouragement.

Mary McDonald, Kintyre, ————, 4, Wilmington North Carolina, For High Rents & better Encouragement.

Jessy McDonald, Kintyre, ————, 2, Wilmington North Carolina, For High Rents & better Encouragement.

Archibald Campbell, Kintyre, Farmer, 38, Wilmington North Carolina, For High Rents & better Encouragement.

Jean McNeil, Kintyre, ————, 32, Wilmington North Carolina, For High Rents & better Encouragement.

Mary Campbell, Kintyre, ————, 7, Wilmington North Carolina, For High Rents & better Encouragement.

Lachlan Campbell, Kintyre, ————, 2, Wilmington North Carolina, For High Rents & better Encouragement.

Girzie Campbell, Kintyre, ————, 6, Wilmington North Carolina, For High Rents & better Encouragement.

Finlay Murchie, Kintyre, Farmer, 45, Wilmington, North Carolina, For High Rents & better Encouragement.

Catherine Hendry, Kintyre, ————, 35, Wilmington North Carolina, For High Rents & better Encouragement.

Archd McMurchy, Kintyre, ————, 10, Wilmington North Carolina, For High Rents & better Encouragement.

Charles McMurchy, Kintyre, ————, 5, Wilmington North Carolina, For High Rents & better Encouragement.

Neil McMurchy, Kintyre, ————, 3, Wilmington North Carolina, For High Rents & better Encouragement.

---

[54] The information in the order given is classified in the original report under the headings: names, former residence, occupation or employment, age, to what port or place bound, on what account and for what purpose.

Barbara McMurchy, Kintyre, ————, ½, Wilmington North Carolina, For High Rents & better Encouragement.

Duncan McRob, Kintyre, Taylor, 26, Wilmington North Carolina, For High Rents & better Encouragement.

Elizabeth McMurchy, Kintyre, ————, 8, Wilmington North Carolina, For High Rents & better Encouragement.

Hugh Sillar, Kintyre, Farmer, 55, Wilmington, North Carolina, For High Rents & better Encouragement.

Catharine Currie, Kintyre, ————, 62, Wilmington North Carolina, For High Rents & better Encouragement.

Mary Sillar, Kintyre, ————, 27, Wilmington North Carolina, For High Rents & better Encouragement.

Catharine Sillar, Kintyre, ————, 23, Wilmington North Carolina, For High Rents & better Encouragement.

Gilbert McKenzie, Kintyre, Farmer, 34, Wilmington North Carolina, For High Rents & better Encouragement.

Mary McKenzie, Kintyre, ————, 27, Wilmington North Carolina, For High Rents & better Encouragement.

Arch^d. McMillan, Kintyre, Farmer, ——, Wilmington North Carolina, For High Rents & better Encouragement.

Patrick McMurchie, Kintyre, Farmer, 17, Wilmington North Carolina, For High Rents & better Encouragement.

Elizabeth Kelso, Kintyre, ————, 50, Wilmington North Carolina, For High Rents & better Encouragement.

Hugh McMurchie, Kintyre, Farmer, 46, Wilmington North Carolina, For High Rents & better Encouragement.

Arch^d McMurchie, Kintyre, Farmer, 21, Wilmington North Carolina, For High Rents & better Encouragement.

Mary McMurchie, Kintyre, ————, 17, Wilmington North Carolina, For High Rents & better Encouragement.

Elizabeth McMurchie, Kintyre, ————, 14, Wilmington North Carolina, For High Rents & better Encouragement.

Robert McMurchie, Kintyre, ————, 9, Wilmington North Carolina, For High Rents & better Encouragement.

Neil Hendry, Kintyre, Taylor, 27, Wilmington North Carolina, For High Rents & better Encouragement.

Coll McAlester, Kintyre, Taylor, 24, Wilmington North Carolina, For High Rents & better Encouragement.

Mary McAlester, Kintyre, ————, 31, Wilmington North Carolina, For High Rents & better Encouragement.

John McVicar, Glasgow, Taylor, 36, Wilmington North Carolina, For High Rents & better Encouragement.

Alexander Speir, Glasgow, Clerk, 19, Wilmington North Carolina, For High Rents & better Encouragement.

Signed { Jo Clerk D Coll^r
         { Alex^r. Campbell D Compt^r

INDEX

Note: Superscript letters have been brought down to the line and the abbreviation has been expanded using brackets. Brackets have also been used to provide further description, a definition, or a variant spelling. Maiden names have been cross-referenced with married names.

A

Achanny, Scotland, 20
Achinnaris, Scotland, 22
Adkins, David (cooper), 7
Adrachoolish/Adrahoolish, Parish of , Scotland, 24
Agriculture, 24
Ajax (ship), 13
Allan, Alex[ande]r (workman), 15
Alpine. *See* Apine
America, 1, 2, 29
Andrews, Thomas (potter), 7
Andrews, William (carpenter), 6
Anson County, N.C., 2
Anthony, John (painter & glazier), 7
Apine, Scotland, 26, 27, 28
Argyle County, Scotland, 2, 13n, 15n, 26n, 28n
Argyleshire, Scotland, 12
Artisans, 2
Aschog [Ascog], Scotland, 21
Auldjo, Alex[ande]r (gentleman), 8
Auldjo, John (gentleman), 8
Ayr, County of (Scotland), 1

B

Bachelor of Leith (ship), 17. See also *Batchelor of Leith*
Baillie, William, 17
Bain, William (widower & shopkeeper), 22
Baker, 6
Bands, Mary (widow), 5
Batchelor of Leith (ship), 25. See also *Bachelor of Leith*
Batty, Eliza[beth] (native of Carolina), 7
Beaton, David (farmer), 15
Beaton, Flora. *See* Bride, Flora
Bedfordshire, England, 5
Belton, Janet (spinster), 5
Besnard, Jno. [Jonathan?] (shipmaster), 3, 6
Bighouse, 18, 24; estate of, 23
Bignell, Jane (servant), 7
Birmingham, England, 5, 7
Black, Ann (child), 28
Black, Christian (child), 28
Black, Donald (laborer), 28
Black, Duncan (child), 28
Black, Ewen (child), 28
Black, Jannet (wife of Donald Black), 28
Black, John (servant), 27
Black, Mary (servant), 27

Blackburn, Benjamin (clergyman), 3
Blackett, Tobiah (spinster), 5
Bladen County, N.C., 2
Blakswik, James (clerk), 4
Blythe, John (gentleman), 9
Bookkeepers, 5, 9
Borgymore, 22
Boston, Ma., 29
Bowie, Ann (servant), 7
Brazier, England, 7
Brazier [brass worker], 7
Bread: high cost of, cited as cause for emigration, 3, 11, 18-21 (passim), 23; price of, increased by distilling, 19
Bride, Chirst (wife of Peter McArthur), 15
Bride, Flora (wife of David Beaton), 15
Briton (ship), 5, 9
Brown, John (bookkeeper), 5
Brown, Katrine (wife of Angus Galbreath), 14
Brown, Samuel (shipmaster), 25
Brunswick, N.C., 10
Buchanan, Arch[ibal]d, 17
Buges, James (merchant), 12
Buges, Marg[aret]. *See* Hog, Marg[aret]
Burntisland, Scotland, 10
Butchers, 5, 8, 9
Butler, Ann (wife of John Butler), 6
Butler, John (gentleman), 6

C

Cabinetmakers, 3, 7
Caithness, County of, 17-24 (passim); emigrants from, 2-3; as Highland county, 2-3
Calewell, Dan[ie]l (shoemaker), 15
Cameron, Allan (farmer), 16
Cameron, Angus (farmer), 16
Cameron, Katrine (wife of Angus Cameron), 16
Campbell, Alex (deputy comptroller), 16, 30
Campbell, Alex[ande]r (child), 20
Campbell, Ann (wife of Robert Mitchell), 15
Campbell, Archibald (farmer), 29
Campbell, Cath[eri]n[e] (wife of Andrew Hyndman), 15
Campbell, Colin, 3
Campbell, Dan[ie]l (farmer), 15
Campbell, Donald (farmer), 24
Campbell, Duncan (child), 25

Campbell, Duncan (collector), 29
Campbell, Girzie (child), 29
Campbell, Hector (child), 20
Campbell, Jean (wife of John McNabb), 12
Campbell, Jean (wife of Robert McNicol), 13
Campbell, Katherine (wife of William Campbell), 25
Campbell, Lachlan (child), 29
Campbell, Mary (child), 29
Campbell, Neil (comptroller), 29
Campbell, Robert (child), 25
Campbell, Ronald, 17
Campbell, William (laborer), 25
Cape Fear, N.C., 2, 8
Carmichael, Allan (child), 27
Carmichael, Archibald (child), 27
Carmichael, Archibald (laborer), 28
Carmichael, Catherine (child), 28
Carmichael, Christian (servant), 27
Carmichael, Dugald (farmer), 27
Carmichael, Evan (laborer), 27
Carmichael, Katherine (child), 27
Carmichael, Margaret (wife of Evan Carmichael), 27
Carmichael, Mary (wife of Archibald Carmichael), 28
Carmichael, Mary (wife of Dugald Carmichael), 27
Carmichail, Donald, 26
Carolina, 3, 9
Carolina (ship), 3, 6
Carolina Packet (ship), 6, 7
Carpenters, 6, 8
Catanoch, John, 18, 19, 22
Cattle: loss of, as cause for emigration, 17-19 (passim),
    24; low price of, as cause for emigration, 3, 18-24;
    rearing of, 28
Chabster/Chapter, 18, 19, 22
Chalmers, James (shipmaster), 13
Chapman, Henry (jeweler), 3
Charterhouse (Edinburgh), 13
Cheshire, S.C., 5
Children, 9, 11, 13-16, 20, 25-30 (passim)
Christy (ship), 12
Clark, James (butcher), 5
Clergyman, 3
Clerk, Jo (deputy collector), 16, 30
Clerks, 3, 4, 6, 8, 9, 24, 30
Clockmaker, 6
Clothier, 25
Clugston, John (collector), 12
Clyne, Parish of, 17
Cochrane, Basil, 13, 17
Collectors, 10, 12, 29
Colquhoun, Ann, 27
Colquhoun, Archibald, 27
Combs, W[illia]m (shipmaster), 4
Commerce (ship), 10
Commissioners of the Customs in Scotland, 13, 17

Comptrollers, 10, 12, 29
Coopers, 5, 7, 10, 15
Coppersmith, 7
Corn, 18, 23, 25; consumption of, in distilling, 21;
    high price of, caused by distilling, 20; increased
    price of, as cause for emigration, 19; scarcity of, as
    cause for emigration, 22; shortage of, 21
Cornwall, England, 3n, 7
Countess of Sutherland. *See* Sutherland, Countess of
County of Ayr. *See* Ayr, County of
County of Caithness. *See* Caithness, County of
County of Strathnaver. *See* Strathnaver, County of
County of Sutherland. *See* Sutherland, County of
Coventry, England, 6
Cowman, Tho[ma]s (shipmaster), 8
Cows, 20, 21
Craigie, Scotland, 21
Crops: destruction of, as cause for emigration, 21;
    failure of, as cause for emigration, 18, 19, 20, 21;
    success of, in America touted, 23
Cumberland County, N.C., 2
Cunningham, Robert (shipmaster), 13
Currie, _____ (shipmaster), 7, 8
Currie, Catharine, 30
Customhouse: in Edinburgh, 10, 13, 17; in London,
    3-9: in Stranraer, 12
Customs officials, 1
Customs, Commissioners of the, 13, 17
Cutting turf, 18

D

Dabzall, Willson (jeweler), 8
Dalrymple, Ann (child), 11
Dalrymple, Arch[ibal]d (child), 11
Dalrymple, Janet (child), 11
Dalrymple, Jas. [James?] (child), 11
Dalrymple, Jean (child), 11
Dalrymple, Jn. [John?] (child), 11
Dalrymple, Jno. [Jonathan?] (farmer), 11
Dalrymple, Mary, 11
Dalrymple, W[illia]m (child), 11
Darby, John (baker), 6
Debts: as cause for emigration, 20, 22
Dee, Robert (gentleman), 8
Delancy, Michael (husbandman), 7
Deputy collectors, 12, 13, 16, 30
Deputy comptrollers, 12, 13, 16, 30
Detlaf, John (tailor), 6
Detlaf, Sarah (wife of John Detlaf), 6
Diana (ship), 29
Distilling, 20, 21; enhanced the price of bread, 3, 19
Dixon, Henry (shipmaster), 9
Dollochcagy, Scotland, 21

Douglas, Alexander (husbandman), 9
Douglas, John (laborer), 10
Downie, Christ[ia]n (wife of Malcolm McPherson), 14
Downie, Joseph (child), 26
Downie, Mary (child), 26
Downie, Mary (wife of John McIntyre), 14
Downy, Christian (spinster), 26
Draper, 8
Drawing master, 5
Drover, 21
Duff, John (herdsman), 12
Duncan, James (farmer), 19
Dundee, [Parish of], 10
Dunlop, John (tide surveyor), 13, 16
Durmmond, John (cooper), 10
Dyer, Joseph (waiter), 8

E

Eastwood, Sarah (spinster), 8
Eckles, John (child), 11
Eckles, W[illia]m (shoemaker), 12
Economic conditions: of North Carolina were less
    attractive than other colonies, 2; poor, as cause for
    emigration to the New World, 2
Edinburgh, Scotland, 10, 13, 17
Edward, Jane (wife of John Edward), 5
Edward, John (farmer), 5
Eglin, Stephen (draper), 8
England, 1, 2, 3-9 (passim)
Evans, Benjamin (sail cloth weaver), 7

F

Factors [middlemen], 19, 21, 22, 23
Falmouth, Port of, 3
Family of Sutherland. *See* Sutherland, Family of
Farmers, 5, 9-11, 14-30 (passim); majority of
    emigrants consisted of, 2
Farms, 3, 18, 19, 23, 24
Farr, Parish of, 18, 19, 22, 23
Ferguson, John (workman), 15
Fife County, 10n
Firth of Forth, 10n
Fishermen, 10
Flatt, James (tailor), 9
Fletcher, Angus (farmer), 14
Fletcher, Euphame (child), 14
Fletcher, Katrine. *See* McIntyre, Katrine
Fletcher, Mary (child), 14
Fletcher, Nancy (child), 14
Forfar County, 10n
Forse, 24

Forsenain, 23
Forster, John (printer), 6
Forsyth, Bezabeer (gentleman), 8
Frasers Regiment, 26, 29
Friendship (ship), 5, 6
Frost, 21, 22

G

Gage, General, 29
Galbreath, Katrine. *See* Brown, Katrine
Galbreath, Angus (workman), 14
Gardener, 8
General Assembly (North Carolina), 2
Gentleman farmer, 26
Gentlemen, 4-6 (passim), 8, 9, 13, 17, 26
Georgia, 12
Gilchrist, Angus (child), 15
Gilchrist, John (cooper), 15
Gilchrist, Marion. *See* Taylor, Marion
Gilks, Edward (leather dresser), 6
Ginnings, Mr. (clerk), 6
Glasgow, Scotland, 12, 13, 30. *See also* Port Glasgow
Glazier, 7
Glenurcha [Glen Orchy], 13, 14
Glenurchy [Glen Orchy], 25, 26
Gordon, Alexander, 17
Gordon, Charles, 18
Gordon, George, 22
Gordon, John, 17
Gordon, Marg[aret], 11
Gordon, William (farmer), 17
Grafton, John (drawing master), 5
Grain, 28
Grant, George (farmer), 21
Grassum [form of payment], 18
Great Britain, 1
Greenlees, John (farmer), 15
Greenlees, Mary. *See* Howie, Mary
Greenock, Port of, 12, 13. *See also* Port Greenock
Groom, 5
Gun, Donald (tailor), 22

H

Halerick, Parish of, 23
Handa Island, 21n. *See also* Islandhanda
Harvest, 18
Hay, 18
Hendry, Catherine, 29
Hendry, Neil (tailor), 30
Herdsman, 12
Herts, England, 5

Highland, 1
Highlanders, 2
Hill, Thomas (joiner), 10
Hindman, Mary (child), 15
Hog, Marg[aret] (wife of James Buges), 12
Hopper, Richard (shipmaster), 8
Horses, 18, 24
Houseman, Henry (gentleman), 8
Howie, Mary (wife of John Greenlees), 15
Howie, Rob[er]t (workman), 14
Huie, Jean (wife of Iver McMillan), 15
Huie, Martha (wife of William Picken), 14
Hull, England, 8
Hunter, Abram (shipmaster), 13
Husbandmen, 4, 7, 9
Husbandry, 23
Hyndman, And[re]w (farmer), 15
Hyndman, Cath[eri]ne. *See* Campbell, Cath[eri]ne
Hyndman, Marg[are]t (child), 15

I

Inch, Scotland, 11, 12
Indented servants, 5-9 (passim)
Inspector generals, 6, 7, 8, 9
Ireland, 7
Island handy (Handa Island), 21
Islandhanda, 23. *See also* Handa Island
Islands of Schetland, 17

J

Jackie of Glasgow (ship), 11
Jamaica Packet (ship), 10
Jamaison, James (farmer & fisherman), 10
James (ship), 8
Jewelers, 3, 7, 8
Joiner, 10, 28
Jupiter of Larne (ship), 25

K

Kabel, Scotland, 23
Kelso, Elizabeth, 30
Kennburgh, James (laborer), 12
Kennburgh, John (laborer), 12
Kenneday, Mary (spinster), 5
Kenneday, William (peruke [wig] maker), 8
Kildonan/Kildonnan, Parish of, 19-22 (passim)
Kinside, Scotland, 22
Kintyre, Scotland, 15, 29, 30

Kirkaldy/Kircaldy, Scotland, 10
Knight, Rob[er]t (planter), 3

L

L'Fabuere, Rachael (lady), 7
Labor: high price of, in America, 19, 20, 21, 23
Laborers, 1, 10-13 (passim), 17, 25-28 (passim)
Ladies, 7, 13
Lairg, Parish of, 20
Lanark County, Scotland, 12n
Land: Carolina had reputation for cheap, 3, 20, 24
Landed gentry, 1
Landlords, 3
Langwall, Scotland, 20
Latheron, Parish of, 24
Le De Spencer (packet boat), 3
Leather dresser, 6
Leicester, England, 7
Leith, Scotland, 10
Lerwick, Port of, 25. *See also* Port Lerwick
Lieutenants, 26, 29
Lincoln, England, 7
Lincolnshire, England, 5
Lismore, Scotland, 28
Literacy, 23
Liverpool, Port of, 5
Loch Ryan, 11n
London (ship), 7, 8
London, Port of, 3-9 (passim)
Lords Commissioners, 13
Lowther (ship), 8
Lyon, James (weaver), 12
Lyon, Mary (wife of Math. Lyon), 12
Lyon, Math. [Matthew?] (weaver), 12

M

Mac Nichol. *See also* McNicol
Mac Nichol, Donald (laborer), 25
Mac Nichol, Katherine (wife of Donald Mac Nichol), 26
MacIntire. *See also* McIntire; McIntyre
MacIntire, Donald (laborer), 25
MacIntire, Katherine (wife of Donald MacIntire), 25
MacIntire, Margaret (child), 25
MacIntire, Mary (child), 25
Mackay, Aeneas, 23
Mackenzie. *See also* McKenzie
Mackenzie, John (clerk & bookkeeper), 9
Macklin, John (gentleman), 4
Macklin, Mary (wife of John Macklin), 4
Magna Charta (ship), 5

Maid, 22

Maitland, R[ichar]d (shipmaster), 5

Malster [maltster], 4

Manufacturing, 1

Margaret & Mary (ship), 4

Marshal, David (clerk), 4

Marshall, John (cooper), 10

Mary & Hannah (ship), 9

Maryland, 1, 2

Maskal, Henry (clerk), 3

Matheson, Hugh (farmer), 20

Matheson, Jas. [James?] (laborer), 11

Matheson, Kathrine (sister of Hugh Matheson), 19

Matheson, Marg[are]t, 11

Mault (Parish of Kildonnan), 19

Maxwell, George Clerk, 13, 17

Maxwell, Rob[er]t (clerk), 8

McAlester, Cath[eri]n[e] (wife of Duncan McAllum), 15

McAlester, Coll (tailor), 30

McAlester, Mary, 30

McAlester, Mary (wife of Malcolm Smith), 15

McAllum. *See also* McCallum

McAllum, Cath[eri]n[e]. *See* McAlester, Cath[eri]n[e]

McAllum, Duncan (shoemaker), 15

McArthur, Ann, 15

McArthur, Cath[eri]n[e] (wife of Malcolm McMullan), 15

McArthur, Chirst. *See* Bride, Chirst

McArthur, Jean, 15

McArthur, John, 15

McArthur, John (child), 15

McArthur, Peter (farmer), 15

McBeath, John (farmer & shoemaker), 19

McBride, Alex[ande]r (laborer), 11

McBride, Arch[ibal]d (child), 11

McBride, Eliz[abeth] (child), 11

McBride, Jas. [James?] (farmer), 11

McBride, Jenny (child), 11

McCallum. *See also* McAllum

McCallum, Duncan (laborer), 28

McCole, Alexander (child), 26

McCole, Ann (child), 28

McCole, Ann (wife of Dugal McCole), 26

McCole, Christian (child), 27, 28

McCole, Christian (wife of Duncan McCole), 27, 28

McCole, David (laborer), 28

McCole, Donald (child), 26

McCole, Donald (laborer), 27

McCole, Dougald (child), 26

McCole, Dugal (laborer), 26

McCole, Dugald, 27

McCole, Duncan, 28

McCole, Duncan (farmer), 27

McCole, Evan (child), 27

McCole, Infant, 26

McCole, John (child), 26

McCole, John (laborer), 26

McCole, Katherine (child), 27

McCole, Katherine (wife of Donald McCole), 27

McCole, Marg[ar]et (child), 26

McCole, Mary, 28

McCole, Mary (child), 26

McCole, Mildred (child), 28

McCole, Mildred (wife of John McCole), 26

McCole, Samuel (child), 26

McCole, Sarah (child), 26, 28

Mcdonald, Alexander, 20

McDonald, Miss Christy (seamstress), 28

McDonald, Donald (farmer & tailor), 19

McDonald, Eliz[abeth] (servant), 19

Mcdonald, George, 20

Mcdonald, Hector (farmer), 20

McDonald, Jessy (child), 29

Mcdonald, John, 20

McDonald, Mary (child), 29

McDonald, William (farmer), 20, 29

McFarlane, Don[al]d (child), 14

McFarlane, Don[al]d (farmer), 14

Mcfarlane, Walter (gentleman), 13

McInish, Ann (child), 27

McInish, Archibald (child), 27

McInish, Catherine (child), 27

McInish, Donald (child), 27

McInish, Jannet (wife of Malcolm McInish), 27

McInish, John, 27

McInish, Malcolm (laborer), 27

McIntire. *See also* MacIntire; McIntyre

McIntire, Ann (spinster), 26

McIntire, Ann (wife of Gilbert McIntire), 27

McIntire, Ann (wife of John McIntire), 26

McIntire, Archibald (child), 26

McIntire, Charles (child), 27

McIntire, Donald (child), 27

McIntire, Duncan (child), 25

McIntire, Duncan (laborer), 28

McIntire, Elizabeth (child), 28

McIntire, Gilbert (tailor), 27

McIntire, John (child), 25, 26, 27

McIntire, John (laborer), 26

McIntire, John (tailor), 27

McIntire, Katherine (child), 28

McIntire, Katherine (wife of Duncan McIntire), 28

McIntire, Katherine (wife of John McIntire), 27

McIntire, Malcolm (child), 27

McIntire, Margaret (child), 26, 27

McIntire, May, 28

McIntire, Polk (comptroller), 12

McIntyre. *See also* MacIntire; McIntire

McIntyre, Christy (child), 14

McIntyre, Don[al]d (child), 14
McIntyre, Donald (farmer), 14
McIntyre, Duncan (farmer), 14
McIntyre, Evan (child), 27
McIntyre, Isobel (wife of Duncan Sinclair), 14
McIntyre, John (child), 14
McIntyre, John (farmer), 14
McIntyre, Katrine (wife of Angus Fletcher), 14
McIntyre, Katrine (wife of Duncan McIntyre), 14
McIntyre, Marg[are]t (wife of John McIntyre), 14
McIntyre, Mary. *See* Downie, Mary
McIntyre, Mary (wife of Donald McIntyre), 14
McIntyre, Nancy (child), 14
McKay, Colonel, 18
McKay, Don[al]d (tailor), 15
McKay, George (tailor & farmer), 22
McKay, James (shoemaker), 25
McKay, William, 18
McKay, Will[ia]m (farmer), 21
McKendrick, Janet (wife of Rob McKichan), 15
McKenzie. *See also* Mackenzie
McKenzie, Gilbert (farmer), 30
McKenzie, Martha, 11
McKenzie, Mary, 30
McKichan, Janet. *See* McKendrick, Janet
McKichan, Neil (child), 15
McKichan, Rob[ert] (farmer), 15
McLaren, Donald (laborer), 28
McLaren, Duncan (laborer), 28
McLaren, Lachlan (laborer), 28
McLarine, Lawrine (joiner), 28
McLeod, Aeneas (farmer), 23
McLeod, Will[ia]m (farmer), 24
McMiken, Janet, 11
McMillan, Arch[ibal]d (child), 15
McMillan, Arc[hibal]d (farmer), 14
McMillan, Arch[ibal]d (farmer), 30
McMillan, Barbra, 14
McMillan, Daniel (farmer), 15
McMillan, Gelb[er]t (child), 15
McMillan, Iver (farmer), 15
McMillan, Jean. *See* Huie, Jean
McMullan, Cath[eri]n[e]. *See* McArthur, Cath[eri]n[e]
McMullan, Mal[col]m (farmer), 15
McMurchie. *See also* McMurchy
McMurchie, Arch[ibal]d (farmer), 30
McMurchie, Elizabeth (child), 30
McMurchie, Hugh (farmer), 30
McMurchie, Mary (child), 30
McMurchie, Patrick (farmer), 30
McMurchie, Robert (child), 30
McMurchy. *See also* McMurchie
McMurchy, Arch[ibal]d (child), 29
McMurchy, Barbara (child), 30
McMurchy, Charles (child), 29

McMurchy, Elizabeth (child), 30
McMurchy, Neil (child), 29
McNabb, Jean. *See* Campbell, Jean
McNabb, John (laborer), 12
McNabb, Tebby, 12
McNeil, Dan[ie]l, 16
McNeil, Hector, 16
McNeil, Isobel. *See* Simpson, Isobel
McNeil, Jean, 29
McNeil, Mary (child), 16
McNeil, Neil (child), 16
McNeil, Neil (farmer), 16
McNeil, Peter, 16
McNeil, Will[ia]m (child), 16
McNicol. *See also* Mac Nichol
McNicol, Angus (laborer), 26
McNicol, Ann (wife of Angus McNicol), 26
McNicol, Annapel (child), 13
McNicol, Archibald (child), 26
McNicol, Jean. *See* Campbell, Jean
McNicol, John (child), 26
McNicol, John (workman), 13
McNicol, Mary (child), 26
McNicol, Nicol (child), 26
McNicol, Robe[r]t (gentleman), 13
McPherson, Christ[ia]n. *See* Downie, Christ[ia]n
McPherson, Janet (child), 14
McPherson, Malcolm (farmer), 14
McPherson, Will[ia]m (child), 14
McQuiston, Jean, 11
McQuiston, Jno. [Jonathan?] (laborer), 11
McRay, George, 21, 23, 24
McRay, W[illia]m (farmer), 24
McRob, Duncan (tailor), 30
McVane, Katherine (spinster), 26
McVey, Doug[ald] (laborer), 12, 13
McVicar, John (deputy comptroller), 13
McVicar, John (tailor), 30
Meal, 19, 20
Menzies, Arch[ibal]d, 13, 17
Menzies, Mary (lady), 13
Merchants, 4-6 (passim), 12, 13
Merks [marks], 17, 18, 23
Middings [manure heaps], 18
Middlesex, England, 5
Milborn, Andrew (child), 9
Milborn, Christopher (child), 9
Mills, Elizabeth, 10
Mills, John (joiner), 10
Ministers, 18, 19, 22
Mitchell, Ann. *See* Campbell, Ann
Mitchell, Rob[er]t (tailor), 15
Mitchell, William (farmer & fisherman), 10
Mointle, Scotland, 19
Molley, Mrs., 6

Mondle, Scotland, 19
Money, currency, 17, 18, 23
Monimia (ship), 13
Monro, Hugh, 20
Monro, Hugh (shoemaker), 24
Monro, Will[ia]m (shoemaker, 22
Morgan, George (farmer), 22
Morison, Alex[ande]r (farmer), 22
Morris, James (shipmaster), 11
Morrison, Edward (shipmaster), 13
Murchie, Finlay (farmer), 29
Murkle, Scotland, 21

N

New England Historical and Genealogical Register, The, 1
New Luce, Scotland, 11, 12
New World, 2
New York, 1, 2, 11, 12, 13
Newcastle, Port of, 8
Newmarket (ship), 8
Nichols, James (silver caster), 7
Nicolson, Mr. Alex[ande]r, 18, 19, 22
North Carolina, 2, 10, 12, 13, 17, 18, 20, 25, 29
North Carolina Historical Commission, 2
Nottingham, England, 7
Nova Scotia, 1

O

Ogier, Catherine (spinster), 4
Ogier, Catherine (wife of Lewis Ogier), 4
Ogier, Charlotte (spinster), 4
Ogier, George (planter), 3
Ogier, John (school boy), 4
Ogier, Lewis (silk throwster), 4
Ogier, Lewis (weaver), 4
Ogier, Lucy (spinster), 4
Ogier, Mary (spinster), 4
Ogier, Peter (school boy), 4
Ogier, Thomas (silk throwster), 4
Oppression: as cause for emigration, 13-16 (passim), 18, 20, 23

P

Packet boat, 3
Painter, 7
Pallas (ship), 6

Parish of Adrachoolish/Adrahoolish. *See* Adrachoolish/Adrahoolish, Parish of
Parish of Clyne. *See* Clyne, Parish of
Parish of Farr. *See* Farr, Parish of
Parish of Halerick. *See* Halerick, Parish of
Parish of Kildonan/Kildonnan. *See* Kildonan/Kildonnan, Parish of
Parish of Lairg. *See* Lairg, Parish of
Parish of Latheron. *See* Latheron, Parish of
Parish of Rae. *See* Rae, Parish of
Parish of Rogart. *See* Rogart, Parish of
Parish of Tongue. *See* Tongue, Parish of
Paton, Philip (comptroller), 10
Peat, 18
Penman, Edward (Ed[ward]) (deputy collector), 12, 13
Pennsylvania, 1, 2
Peruke maker [wig maker], 8
Philips, R. E.: letter to John Robinson from, 10, 12, 13
Picken, Martha. *See* Huie, Martha
Picken, Will[ia]m (farmer), 14
Planter, 3
Plowing, 18
Polly (ship), 5
Pond, Capt. (shipmaster), 3
Population, 1
Port Glasgow, 10. *See also* Glasgow
Port Greenock, 12, 16, 29. *See also* Greenock, Port of
Port Kirkaldy. *See* Kirkaldy
Port Lerwick, 17, 18. *See also* Lerwick, Port of
Port of Falmouth. *See* Falmouth, Port of
Port of Greenock. *See* Greenock, Port of
Port of Lerwick. *See* Lerwick, Port of
Port Stranraer, 11, 12
Ports, 1, 10, 12, 13, 16, 17,18, 25, 29
Potatoes, 25
Potter, 7
Poverty: as cause for emigration, 14, 15, 22
Printer, 6
Provisions: low price of, in America, 20, 21, 23
Public Record Office, 1

R

Rae, Lord, 23, 25
Rae, Parish of, 18, 19, 21-24 (passim)
Ramage, Alex[ande]r (shipmaster), 25
Rea, Estate of, 24
Reading, England, 6
Recruitment, 2
Rellie, Hugh (shipmaster), 12
Renfrew County, Scotland, 10n
Rent: increase of, as cause for emigration, 3, 10, 11, 13-24 (passim), 28, 29, 30; policy of, oppressive, 1
Richardson, Ralph (gardener), 8

Rimsdale, Scotland, 20
Ripley, William (farmer), 9
Risquebah [whiskey], 19
River Clyde, 10n, 12n
Rixon, John (brazier & coppersmith), 7
Robinson, John: letter from Commissioners of the
    Customs in Scotland to, 13, 17; letter from R. E.
    Philips to, 1, 10, 12
Rockingham (ship), 8
Rogart, Parish of, 20
Rose, Robert (planter), 3
Rosehall, Scotland, 17
Ross, John (widower & farmer), 23
Ross, Patrick (schoolmaster), 22
Royal Highland Regiment, 2
Ruthven, Dugald (shipmaster), 29

S

Saddler, 5
Sail cloth weaver, 7
Sanderson, John (farmer), 9
Savall, Scotland, 20
Schetland, 10
Schetland, Islands of, 17. *See also* Shetland Islands
School boys, 4
Schoolmaster, 22
Schools, 22
Scotch Highlanders, 2
Scotland, 4, 5, 8, 9, 11n, 12n, 13; Commissioners of
    the Customs in, 17; customs officials in, 1; poor
    economic conditions in, as cause for emigration to
    the New World, 2; population movement from, 1
Scott, Margaret (spinster), 4
Scott, William (malster), 4
Scouler, Jasper (carpenter), 8
Seamstress, 28
Secretary of the Treasury, 1
Servant boy, 22
Servant maid, 22
Servants, 7, 10, 17, 18, 19, 22, 24, 26, 27
Servants, indented, 1, 2, 5-9 (passim)
Sewing, 25
Shathaledale, Scotland, 24
Sheep, 3
Shepherds, 28
Shetland Islands, 1. *See also* Schetland, Islands of
Shipmasters, 3-13 (passim), 25, 27, 29
Ships, 1, 3-13 (passim), 17, 25, 29
Shire of Sutherland. *See* Sutherland, Shire of
Shoemakers, 12, 15, 17, 19, 22, 24, 25, 26
Shopkeeper, 22
Silk throwsters, 3, 4
Sillar, Catharine, 30

Sillar, Hugh (farmer), 30
Sillar, Mary, 30
Silver caster, 7
Sim, Jane (wife of William Sim), 4
Sim, William (husbandman), 4
Simpson, Isobel (wife of Neil McNeil), 16
Simpson, William (cooper), 5
Sinclair, Alex[ander] (farmer), 21
Sinclair, Ann (spinster), 26
Sinclair, Duncan (farmer), 14
Sinclair, Isobel. *See* McIntyre, Isobel
Sinclair, James (farmer), 23
Sinclair, Sir John, 21
Sinclair, John (farmer), 14
Sinclair, Margarit (spinster), 26
Sinclair, Mary (wife of John Sinclair), 14
Skelpick, Scotland, 18
Smith, Christopher (husbandman), 9
Smith, Esther (wife of Christopher Smith), 9
Smith, James (painter & glazier), 7
Smith, John (cabinetmaker), 7
Smith, John (shipmaster), 5, 6
Smith, Mal[col]m (farmer), 15
Smith, Mary (child), 15
Smith, Mary. *See* McAlester, Mary
Smith, Peter, 15
Smith, Thomas (shipmaster), 10
Soldiers, 18
South Carolina, 5, 8, 10
Southwark, England, 5
Speir, Alexander (clerk), 30
Spinning, 25
Spinsters, 4, 5, 6, 8, 26
Stead, Thomas (butcher), 8
Steven, Chr[istia]n, 11
Steven, Jas. [James?] (farmer), 11
Steven, Sarah (child), 11
Steven, Tho[ma]s (child), 11
Stewart, Alexander (child), 26, 27
Stewart, Alexander (gentleman farmer), 26
Stewart, Allan (lieutenant), 26
Stewart, Captain Allan (former lieutenant), 29
Stewart, Archibald (shoemaker), 26
Stewart, Banco (child), 27
Stewart, Charles (child), 26
Stewart, Christian (child), 27
Stewart, Dougald (laborer), 26
Stewart, Elizabeth (child), 25
Stewart, Elizabeth (wife of John Stewart), 25
Stewart, Isobel (wife of Kenneth Stewart), 27
Stewart, James (child), 26
Stewart, Janet (child), 25
Stewart, John (child), 25, 26, 27
Stewart, John (clothier), 25
Stewart, Kenneth (shipmaster), 27

Stewart, Lilly (child), 26
Stewart, Margaret (child), 25
Stewart, Patrick (child), 25
Stewart, Thomas (child), 26
Stewart, William (child), 27
Stranraer, Port. *See* Port Stranraer
Strathalidale, Scotland, 18
Strathnaver, County of, 18, 25
Strathoolie, Scotland, 22
Surgeon, 13
Surry, England, 6, 8
Surveyor, tide, 13, 16
Sutherland, John, 24
Sutherland, W[illia]m, 18
Sutherland, Will[ia]m, 19
Sutherland, Countess of, 18
Sutherland, County of, 2, 17, 19-24 (passim)
Sutherland, Estate of, 19, 22, 23
Sutherland, Family of, 18
Sutherland, Shire of, 19
Switzerland, 9

T

Tacksmen, 17, 21, 23
Tailors, 6, 9, 15, 19, 22, 27, 30
Taverner, George (groom), 5
Taxes, 2
Taylor, Marion (wife of John Gilchrist), 16
Taylor, Mary (wife of Archibald McMillan), 14
Teacher, 24
Templeman, William (jeweler), 7
Tenants, 18, 21
Thompson, Isaac (shipmaster), 8
Thomson, Neil (farmer), 15
Thurso, Scotland, 18, 19, 22
Tide surveyor, 13, 16
Tomkyns, Jno. [Jonathan?], 3-9 (passim)
Tong, Miss (spinster), 6
Tongue, Parish of, 22, 23, 24
Tradesmen, 29
Treasury, Lords Commissioners of the, 13
Treasury, Secretary of the, 1
Trenham, James (butcher), 9
Turf, cutting, 18
Turner, J. (shipmaster), 6
Tzatt, Sam[ue]l (shipmaster), 4

U

Ulysses (ship), 12, 13
Union (ship), 4
Urquhart, Alex[ande]r (shipmaster), 5, 9

V

Vernan, Thomas (silk throwster), 3
Virginia, 1, 2

W

Wages: Carolina had reputation for high, 3; low, as
    cause for emigration, 3, 10
Waiter, 8
Walker, Cath[e]r[ine], 11
Walker, William (merchant), 5
War, 2
Weather, 17, 21, 22
Weavers, 4, 7, 12, 17
Wescott, Philip (shipmaster), 7
West, John (gentleman), 8
Weston, Ann (lady), 7
Wheat, 25
White, John (shipmaster), 6, 7
White, Sarah (merchant), 6
Whyt, Robert (collector), 10
Wick, Scotland, 22
Widow, 5
Widowers, 22, 23
Wig maker, 8
Wigtown County, 11n
William (ship), 7
Williams, John (cabinetmaker), 3
Williamson, Andrew (farmer & fisherman), 10
Wilmington, N.C., 13, 17-20, 23-25 (passim), 29, 30
Wilson, David (merchant), 4
Wilson, Gilbert (shipmaster), 8
Wilson, James (saddler), 5
Wilson, James (shipmaster), 12
Wilson, William (planter), 3
Winship, Thomas (clockmaker), 6
Winter, Thomas (husbandman), 7
Worker, Nathaniel (gentleman), 5
Workmen, 13, 14, 15
Wright, Isobel, 29
Wymore, Scotland, 17

Y

York, England, 9
Yorkshire, England, 5
Young, Thomas (surgeon), 13